VISUAL QUICKSTART GUIDE

QUICKEN 98

FOR MACINTOSH

Tom Negrino

Peachpit Press

Visual QuickStart Guide
Quicken 98 for Macintosh
Tom Negrino

Peachpit Press
1249 Eighth Street
Berkeley, CA 94710
510/524-2178
800/283-9444
510/524-2221 fax

Find us on the World Wide Web at: http://www.peachpit.com

Peachpit Press is a division of Addison Wesley Longman

Editor: Marjorie Baer
Copyeditor: Lisa Theobald
Production Coordinator: Kate Reber
Cover design: The Visual Group
Compositor: Melanie Haage
Indexer: Valerie Robbins

ISBN 0-201-35401-2

0 9 8 7 6 5 4 3

Printed and bound in the United States of America

♻ Printed on recycled paper

Dedication

To my father Joseph Negrino, who has touched so many people's lives, becoming more than their accountant; he's become their friend. Thanks for the inspiration, Dad.

Special Thanks to:

The folks at Peachpit:

My editor, Marjorie Baer, for making this a wonderful experience. I knew it would be.

Lisa Theobald, who has restored my faith in copy editors. Thanks especially for the captions.

Nancy Ruenzel, for believing in the project.

Nancy Davis, the book's (formerly) pregnant midwife.

The people at Intuit:

Adam Samuels, who got behind and pushed when necessary.

Russell Florez, the man with the answers.

I'd also like to thank my agent, StudioB's David Rogelberg, and Sherry Rogelberg, AKA She Who Makes the Checks Flow.

Thanks to Suzy Prieto, for her patience and Sean Smith, for being the World's Best Kid™.

Thanks always to Dori Smith, for her love and incredible support. And for the Little Chocolate Donuts at just the right time.

FOREWORD

What do Macintosh, the best personal computer on the planet, and Quicken, the best-selling personal finance program, have in common? Passion, for one thing. Customers like you (and me) treat their Macs and Quicken with affection and enthusiasm. We don't just like these products—we love them.

It's fitting, then, that Apple and Intuit have come together to deliver the latest release of Quicken for Macintosh— Quicken Deluxe 98—as part of Apple's revolutionary new iMac computer. Together, these products can help you become even more powerful when it comes to taking control of your finances. When combined with the power of Quicken.com, the leading personal finance Web site, you'll find new ways to get your financial life organized, eliminate hassle, and save time and money.

Peachpit Press couldn't have found a more passionate guide to the world of Quicken for Macintosh than Tom Negrino. He's illuminated the world of Mac software for years, as a longtime contributor to *Macworld* and *MacAddict* magazines. He's spent years as a member and leader of the Los Angeles Macintosh Group. And, of course, he's a loyal and longtime Quicken user.

You're in excellent hands.

Adam Samuels
Product Manager
Quicken for Macintosh
Intuit, Inc.

TABLE OF CONTENTS

TABLE OF CONTENTS

TABLE OF CONTENTS

TABLE OF CONTENTS

INTRODUCTION

Money pervades our lives, simultaneously desired and disdained. Most of us can't get along without it and would love to have more of it. Yet many of us don't do an especially good job of managing the money that we do have. How often have you heard people say things like "I don't know where all my money goes"? Many people live from paycheck to paycheck, just getting along with no financial plan for the future and hardly any control over their financial present.

Sound familiar? It certainly does to me; I was one of those people for many years. I finally got fed up with feeling that my finances were out of my control, so one December evening I bought a copy of Quicken Deluxe and promised myself that I would start using it when the new year began. I did start using it, and melodramatic as it sounds, it changed my life. I used Quicken to take stock of my finances, then I came up with a plan to pay off my debts and start saving for the future. Today I'm happy to say that I no longer wonder what my financial picture is, because Quicken gives me all the information that I need.

If you want to get better control over your finances, this book is for you. I'll show you how to use Quicken to help you get out of debt, manage your present finances, and invest for the future.

Welcome, iMac Owners!

I'd especially like to welcome aboard owners of Apple's cool iMac computer. In fact, you folks are one of the main reasons this book was written; when I found out that every iMac would include a copy of Quicken Deluxe, I suggested to my editors at Peachpit Press that iMac owners deserved a book about Quicken that was as friendly as the iMac itself. Luckily, they had the good sense to agree.

Just the Facts, Ma'am

I have to admit that I don't have a lot of patience for computer books that are thick and heavy enough to cause injury if you accidentally drop them on your foot. I'd rather open a book, find out how to do a task, and toss the book back on the shelf without wading through endless blather and more details than I ever wanted to know.

In this book, I've organized different financial tasks into chapters, and within each chapter are step-by-step directions that tell you exactly how to accomplish various tasks.

On occasion, you'll see this icon. It points out the differences between Quicken 98 and Quicken Deluxe 98. Whenever you see the icon, it means that the feature being discussed is only in Quicken Deluxe 98.

My Assumptions About You

In writing this book, I've made the following assumptions about you. First, you own either Quicken 98 or Quicken Deluxe 98 and a Macintosh powerful enough to run the programs. That's not a difficult requirement, as Quicken will run on machines using 68030 processors, with between 8 MB and 16 MB of RAM, running System 7.1 or higher. That pretty much means that if your Macintosh was built anytime after about 1992, chances are it will run Quicken just fine.

I've also made the assumption that you're familiar with the basics of using a Macintosh. You don't need be a Mac guru, but you shouldn't be stumped by concepts like selecting text, clicking and dragging, and using files and folders. If you need to brush up on the essentials, allow me to suggest that you pick up a copy of the excellent *Mac OS 8.5: Visual QuickStart Guide*, by Maria Langer, coincidentally also published by Peachpit Press.

Last, I've made the assumption that if you have bought this book, you're a person of uncommon discernment, style, and grace. If you're just leafing through these pages in a bookstore, I'm trusting you not to let me down.

What's Not in This Book

Because I wanted to write a book that was genuinely useful, rather than one that slavishly touched every base and documented every Quicken feature, I had to decide what I didn't want to put in the book. So I looked through Quicken for features that were little used or that weren't that great. The first feature to get the heave-ho was Budgeting. Making budgets is one of those things that everyone says they want to do, but hardly anyone really does. This isn't just my opinion; I've seen surveys of real Quicken users that bear me out. My apologies to you if you are one of the few, the proud, who really do use budgets. A close relative to Budgeting is Forecasting, which also did not make the cut.

While I've included two chapters on investments, those chapters are intended for the relatively light-duty investor. If you have a modest stock portfolio, some mutual funds, and some other savings plans, the investment chapters should work just fine for you. But it you're constantly churning your portfolio, buying and selling options, and otherwise serious about playing the markets, you might find my investment chapters to be a bit thin.

I've also skipped over some of the less-interesting of Quicken's companion programs, such as the Refinance calculator and the Quicken Home Inventory program, the latter of which is one of the few outright flops in the otherwise-excellent Quicken package.

Let's get started

A popular bit of philosophy states that "The journey is the reward." I'm afraid that my pragmatic side says that when it comes to money, I believe that "The reward is the reward." In this case, the reward of using Quicken can mean smarter control over your finances, and in turn a better and richer life for yourself and for your family. That's a journey well worth taking. Thanks for joining me.

Tom Negrino

July 1998

INTRODUCING QUICKEN 98

Welcome to Quicken 98! In this chapter, you'll learn how to start Quicken, convert old Quicken files (if you've been using an older version of the program), use Quicken's interface, ask Quicken for help, and customize Quicken so that it works the way you do.

Running Quicken for the First Time

To launch Quicken 98:

1. Double-click the Quicken folder on your hard disk.

2. Double-click the Quicken Deluxe 98 or the Quicken 98 icon in the Quicken folder (**Figure 1.1**).

3. Quicken starts and displays a tip (**Figure 1.2**).

To convert old Quicken files:

1. Choose File > Open File. The open file dialog appears (**Figure 1.5**).

2. Navigate to the old Quicken file, select it, and click the Open button.

3. Quicken converts your old file into the current version's format. The process is irreversible, but Quicken saves a backup copy of your old data file in a folder called Old Quicken Data.

✔ Tips

- If you don't want a tip to show up when you launch Quicken, choose Edit > Preferences and then click the General icon in the scrolling area on the left (**Figure 1.3**). Then clear the "Show Tip at startup" check box and click the OK button.

- After Quicken 98 has successfully converted your previous version data file, it's important that you remove old versions of Quicken from your hard disk. You won't want to accidentally open your Quicken 98 file with an older version of Quicken because you're likely to corrupt your data.

Quicken Deluxe 98

Figure 1.1 Double-click the Quicken icon to start the program.

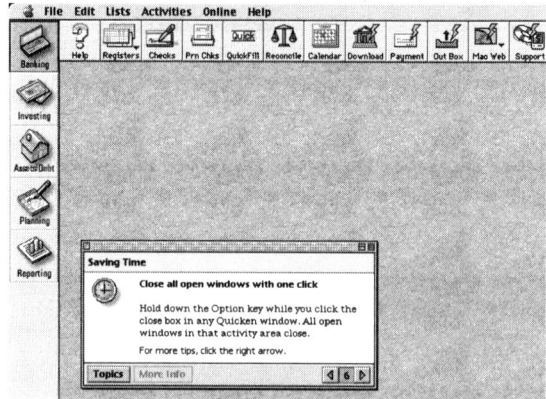

Figure 1.2 To learn more about Quicken, read a new tip each time you start the program.

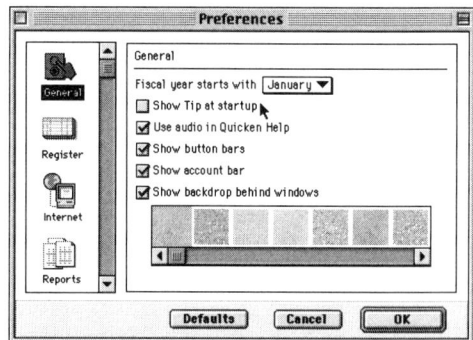

Figure 1.3 Clear the "Show Tip at startup" check box in the Preferences window to keep Tips from showing up.

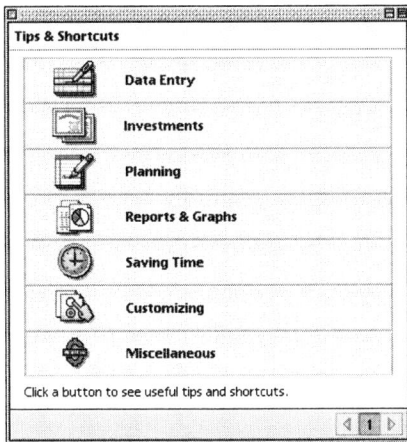

Figure 1.4 Browse through all Quicken's tips in the Tips & Shortcuts window, accessible from the Help menu.

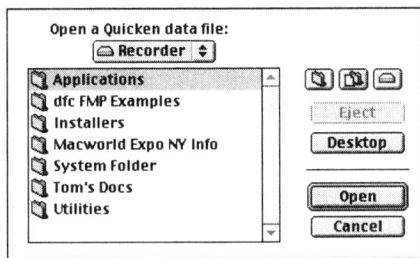

Figure 1.5 The Open File dialog helps you find files that you want to open.

Figure 1.6 Use the activity areas bar to move among different financial tasks.

Finding Your Way Around

There are a lot of features in Quicken, so to make it easier to use, the program is divided into five main sections called *activity areas*, which are displayed along the left side of the screen. At the top of the screen is the *menu bar*, where you'll find all of Quicken's commands. Right below the menu bar is another bar of buttons called the *task bar*. The buttons in the task bar change depending on which activity area you're working in.

Activity areas

Each button on the left side of the screen represents a different activity area (**Figure 1.6**). Each area represents a different financial task.

- The **Banking** area lets you work with different bank accounts, including checking, savings, and money-market accounts.

- In the **Investing** area, you'll track stocks, bonds, mutual funds, and other investments in your portfolio.

- In the **Assets/Debt** section, you can deal with credit cards, loans, mortgages, and assets such as your home.

- **Planning** lets you budget and forecast your finances and figure out how to get out of debt, and its calculators can help you plan for your retirement.

- The **Reports** area lets you create reports and graphs to show what's happening with your money.

✔ Tip

- To see Tips at any time, choose Help > Tips & Shortcuts to open a window with Tips topics (**Figure 1.4**).

The menu bar

There isn't much to say about the menu bar (**Figure 1.7**); as with any Mac program, the commands Quicken needs to do your bidding are located on the menus.

The task bar

The task bar (**Figure 1.8**) provides another way to choose Quicken commands. The task bar changes depending on the activity area that you are working in. You can click a button on the task bar to tell Quicken to perform some action.

The backdrop

To reduce confusion between Quicken's windows and windows in the Finder, Quicken hides the Finder and other applications behind the backdrop. If you want to get to the Finder, click in the dog-eared part of the backdrop at the lower right corner of the screen.

✔ Tip

- If you're using a small monitor, click the bottom of the activity areas bar to toggle between icons and text. Then click and drag in the text area to turn the activity areas bar into a floating text palette that takes up less room on your screen (**Figure 1.9**).

File Edit Lists Activities Online Help

Figure 1.7 You can tell Quicken where to go and what to do from the menu bar.

Figure 1.8 The task bar is a good alternative for the "menu-impaired."

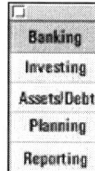

Figure 1.9 When you're short of screen real-estate, turn the activity areas bar into a floating text palette.

Banking
Investing
Assets/Debt
Planning
Reporting

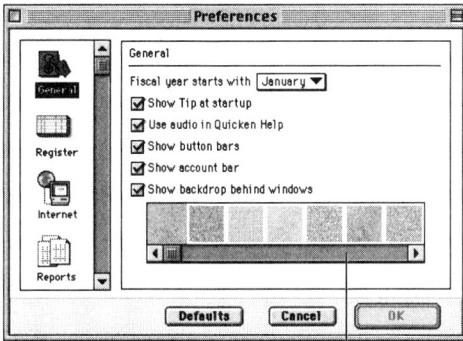

Scrolling backdrop
color area

Figure 1.10 Use the Preferences dialog to change the behavior of the backdrop or the button bars.

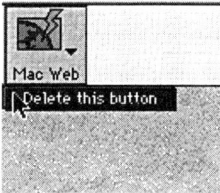

Figure 1.11 Click "Delete this button" to delete a button from the task bar.

Customizing Your Workspace

Quicken gives you a variety of ways to customize the program to your personal style.

To change or eliminate the backdrop and button bars:

1. Choose Edit > Preferences, and then click the General icon (**Figure 1.10**).

2. To change the color of the backdrop, scroll in the horizontal color area near the bottom of the window, select a color by clicking on it, and then click the OK button.

3. To eliminate the backdrop, clear the "Show backdrop behind windows" check box and then click the OK button.

4. To get rid of the button bars, clear the "Show button bars" check box and then click the OK button.

To remove a button from the task bar:

1. Hold down the Control and Option keys, and then click and hold down the mouse button on the task bar button that you want to remove. A small menu that says "Delete this button" will appear below the button (**Figure 1.11**).

2. Choose the "Delete this button" item. The button disappears from the task bar.

To move a button on the task bar:

1. Hold down the Option key and click on the button that you want to move.

2. Drag the button to its new home.

CUSTOMIZE YOUR WORKSPACE

To add a button to the task bar:

1. At the far right edge of the task bar, click the Library button (**Figure 1.12**). The Task Button Library window appears (**Figure 1.13**).

2. Click on the tab to view the menu that includes the command you want to add.

3. Drag the button from the Task Button Library window to its new location on the task bar.

To create your own Command-key shortcuts:

1. Hold down the Command key and click in the menu bar. The mouse cursor turns into the command symbol. Don't release the mouse button.

2. Let go of the Command key and select the menu command to which you want to assign the shortcut.

3. With the command selected, release the mouse button. The Edit Command Key window appears (**Figure 1.14**) and shows you the name of the menu command and the existing shortcut (if one exists).

4. Type in the key that will be combined with the Command key, and then click the OK button. If another menu command already uses the same shortcut key, Quicken will ask you to confirm your change. If you confirm, Quicken removes the shortcut from the other command and assigns the shortcut to the key you've selected.

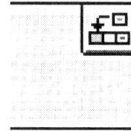

Figure 1.12 Choose the Library button to add buttons to the task bar.

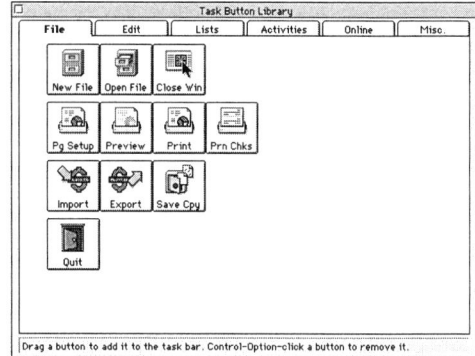

Figure 1.13 The Task Button Library window lets you drag buttons onto the task bar.

Figure 1.14 Use the Edit Command Key window to change any Command-key shortcut.

Help
About Quicken Help
Show Balloons
Quicken Help   ⌘?
Tips & Shortcuts
Quicken Basics
User's Manual

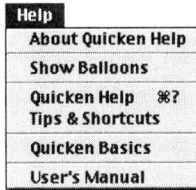

Figure 1.15 Use Quicken's Help menu to get help fast.

Getting On-Screen Help

Quicken provides several options for on-screen help (although none are as wonderful as this book, naturally). Not surprisingly, you get to the program's help files via the Help menu (**Figure 1.15**).

About Quicken Help

Choose About Quicken Help to see an overview screen that shows you the different ways to get help (**Figure 1.16**). Click one of the buttons to find out more about that particular help option.

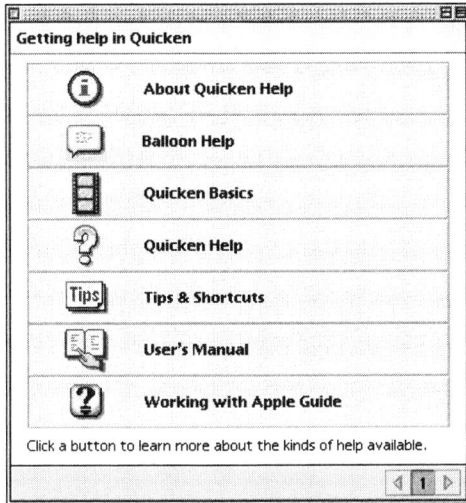

Balloon Help

Choose Show Balloons from the Help menu to turn on Balloon Help, which shows you descriptions of items when you point at them (**Figure 1.17**). Balloon Help is useful to help you learn about unfamiliar features, but you'll probably grow tired of the balloons popping up everywhere you move the mouse. To turn off Balloon Help, choose Hide Balloons from the Help menu.

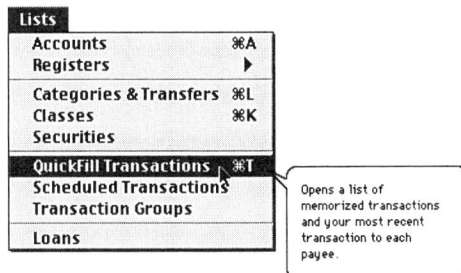

Getting help in Quicken

- (i) About Quicken Help
- Balloon Help
- Quicken Basics
- Quicken Help
- Tips & Shortcuts
- User's Manual
- Working with Apple Guide

Click a button to learn more about the kinds of help available.

Figure 1.16 To get an overview of Quicken's help options, choose About Quicken Help from the Help menu.

Lists
Accounts	⌘A
Registers	▸
Categories & Transfers	⌘L
Classes	⌘K
Securities	
QuickFill Transactions	⌘T
Scheduled Transactions	
Transaction Groups	
Loans	

Opens a list of memorized transactions and your most recent transaction to each payee.

Figure 1.17 Balloon Help is useful in small doses, but it can get tedious as you get to know your way around. When you don't need Balloon Help, choose Hide Balloons to turn it off.

Quicken Help

Quicken Help gives you step-by-step instructions on how to accomplish tasks. The Quicken Help window is divided into topic areas (**Figure 1.18**). This is the best help tool to use for learning new tasks.

Tips & Shortcuts

These quick-tip topics (**Figure 1.19**) help you get more out of Quicken and show you how to accomplish tasks more quickly and easily.

Quicken Basics

From this window, you can select one of eight QuickTime movies that show you how to accomplish various financial tasks (**Figure 1.20**).

User's Manual

Select this item to open the Quicken User's Manual in Adobe Acrobat format.

To quit Quicken:

1. Choose File > Quit.

2. Quicken will close all open windows and return you to the Finder. You don't have to worry about saving your work because Quicken automatically saves your work for you.

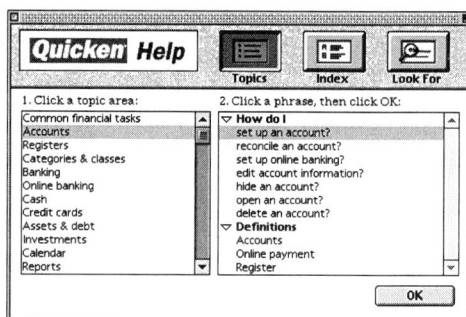

Figure 1.18 Quicken Help is the best way to learn unfamiliar tasks.

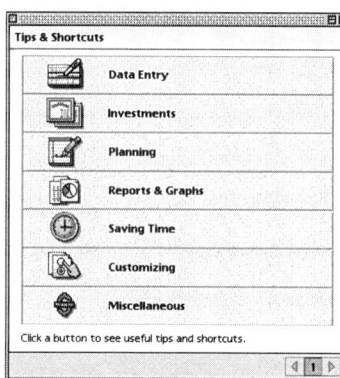

Figure 1.19 Reading Tips & Shortcuts will make Quicken easier to use.

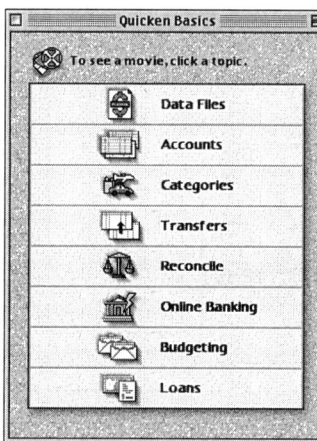

Figure 1.20 Quicken Basics QuickTime movies teach you the basics of eight financial tasks.

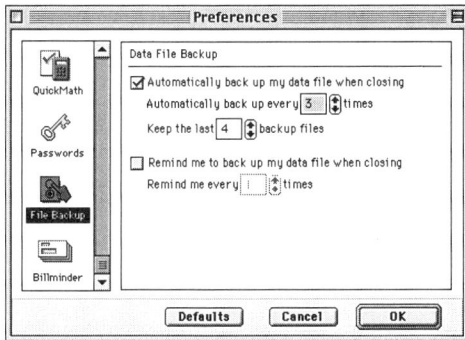

Figure 1.21 It's a good idea to set Quicken to automatically back up your data file.

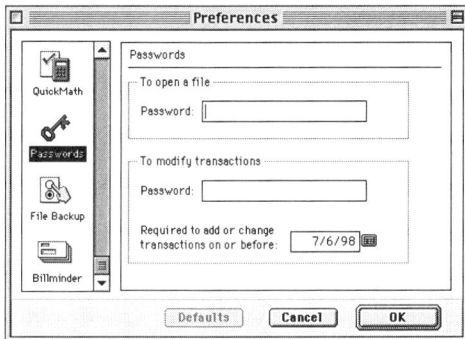

Figure 1.22 You can protect your data file from casual browsing by setting a password. But don't forget it!

To have Quicken automatically back up your data file:

1. Choose Edit > Preferences. The Preferences window appears.

2. In the scrolling area at the left edge of the Preferences window, scroll down and click the File Backup icon (**Figure 1.21**).

3. Click the "Automatically back up my data file when closing" check box.

4. Click the OK button.

To protect your data file with a password:

1. Choose Edit > Preferences. The Preferences window appears.

2. In the scrolling area at the left edge of the window, scroll down and click the Passwords icon (**Figure 1.22**).

3. To require use of a password when opening a file, enter a password in the "To open a file" box.

4. To require use of a password when changing a transaction, enter a password in the "To modify transactions" box.

5. Click the OK button.

✔ Tip

- Warning! If you forget your password(s), the only way to get access to your data is to send your entire data file to Intuit. The company's crack team of code breakers will remove your passwords. Intuit will also charge you a fee for the service.

GETTING ON-SCREEN HELP

What's the Difference Between Quicken Basic 98 and Quicken Deluxe 98?

Quicken Deluxe 98, which is bundled with the Apple iMac computer and also sold separately, includes these useful additions to the basic Quicken 98 product:

- QuickEntry is a mini application that lets you enter transactions into any Quicken account without opening Quicken itself. For more on QuickEntry, see Chapter 4.

- The Emergency Records Organizer application saves your personal information in one place.

- The Quicken Home Inventory program helps you keep an inventory of your possessions.

- The Tax Deduction Finder steps you through a simple questionnaire that helps determine whether you might qualify for additional tax deductions.

- You can obtain a free copy of your credit report.

- The Debt Reduction Planner evaluates your debt level and steps you through creation of an action plan to get you out of debt faster.

- The Retirement Planner helps you create a plan to reach your retirement goals.

- In the Net Worth Analysis, you'll get a snapshot of your financial health.

- Quicken Basics are QuickTime tutorials that teach you about various Quicken tasks.

- The on-screen User's Manual in Adobe Acrobat format gives you quick answers.

QUICKEN BASIC VS. QUICKEN DELUXE

2

Setting Up Accounts

Quicken stores all of your information in a *data file* on your hard disk, which you create the first time you use the program. You need only one data file, but inside the data file you'll create a number of *accounts*. An account represents an *asset* (something that you own, such as the money in your checking account or some property) or a *liability* (a debt that you owe, such as the balance on your credit cards or a mortgage).

Quicken allows you to have as many or as few accounts as you wish (actually, the upper limit is 255 accounts, but most people won't use more than a couple dozen accounts). Some people prefer to use Quicken to track only their main checking account, and other people create many accounts to track every penny.

In this chapter, you'll set up your data file and learn about the different account types within Quicken.

Creating a Data File

The first time you run Quicken, you'll need to create a data file to contain all your financial information. A data file must include at least one account, so you will create your checking account immediately after you create the data file.

To create a new data file and checking account:

1. Choose File > New File. The New File dialog box will appear, asking if you're sure that you want to create a new data file (**Figure 2.1**). Click OK. The Save dialog box appears (**Figure 2.2**).

2. Navigate to where you want to save your data file, and then enter a name for the file in the "File for your Quicken data" box. You can include Quicken's standard home or business *categories* in your data file. Categories are labels that you assign to your transactions that help you track where your money comes from and where it goes. Choose the Home or Business check box (or both), and then click the New button. The Set Up Account window appears (**Figure 2.3**).

3. Select the Bank radio button. You use this radio button to set up checking, savings, or money-market accounts.

4. Enter a name for your checking account.

5. Enter a description for the checking account (optional).

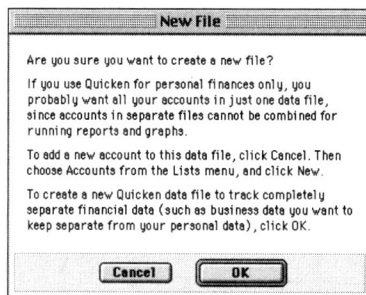

Figure 2.1 Reassure Quicken that you indeed want to create a new file by clicking the OK button.

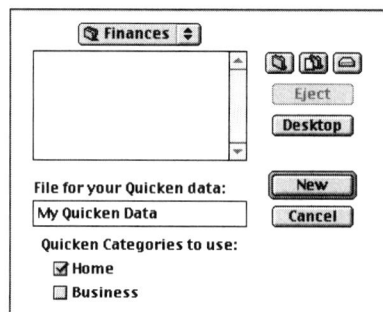

Figure 2.2 Choose where you want to save your data file in the Save dialog box.

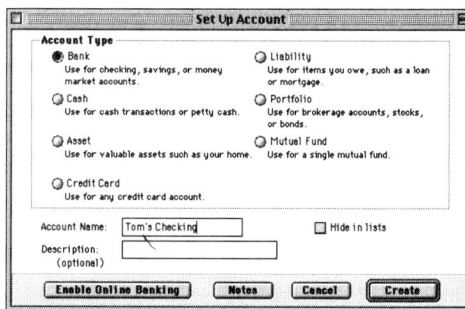

Figure 2.3 Create a new account in the Set Up Account window.

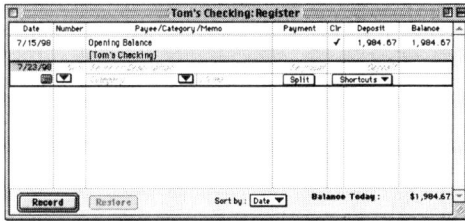

Figure 2.4 Enter checking account data in your new account register.

Figure 2.5 After you create a new account, it appears in the Accounts window.

6. Click the Create button. Quicken creates the account and opens a register for the new checking account (**Figure 2.4**), ready for you to enter the opening balance in the Deposit field. Type the ending balance from your last bank statement into the Deposit field, and then press the Tab key until the Date field is highlighted. Type in the last statement date, and then click the Record button (or press the Enter key).

7. Quicken opens the Accounts window that lists your new checking account name, the account type, and the account balance (**Figure 2.5**).

✔ Tip

■ Whenever you click the Record button, Quicken saves your work, so you don't need to worry about saving before you quit the program.

Using Accounts

Quicken has five kinds of accounts that you can use to track your assets:

- The **Bank** account tracks checking accounts, savings accounts, money-market accounts, and debit cards. This is the only account type you can use to make electronic payments or to write checks.

- The **Asset** account tracks the value of an asset, such as real estate or your car.

- The **Portfolio** account tracks brokerage accounts that contain financial instruments, such as stocks and bonds.

- A **Mutual Fund** account tracks a single mutual fund.

- The **Cash** account is unlike the rest of the accounts because no corresponding account exists in a financial institution. You use the Cash account to track out-of-pocket expenses. For example, let's say that you withdraw $100 from an ATM. In Quicken, that amount comes out of your checking account and goes into the Cash account. As you spend the money, you can make notations in the Cash account to track how that money has been spent.

Quicken also has two account types to track your liabilities:

- **Credit card** accounts can track your credit cards, equity lines, and other lines of credit.

- **Liability** accounts are usually loans, such as a mortgage or car loan.

Figure 2.6 Click the Banking button to switch to Quicken's banking transaction area.

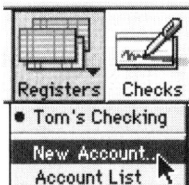

Figure 2.7 Choose New Account from the Registers pop-up menu to start creating a new account.

To create a new account:

1. Click the Banking button in the activity bar (**Figure 2.6**).

2. From the Registers pop-up menu in the task bar, choose New Account (**Figure 2.7**). The Set Up Account window appears (refer to **Figure 2.3**).

3. Select the radio button corresponding to the kind of account you wish to create, type in an account name, and enter a description (optional). Click the Create button.

4. Quicken creates the account, adds its name to the Account list in the Accounts window, and opens its register.

5. Enter an opening balance, and if necessary change the date. See **Table 2.1** for guidance on which amounts and dates to use for opening balances.

Table 2.1

Entering Opening Balances		
ACCOUNT TYPE	OPENING BALANCE	DATE
Bank	New balance from your last bank statement	Date of your last statement
Credit card	New balance from your last statement	Date of your last statement
Asset	The asset's current value	Today's date
Liability	The liability's current value	Today's date
Portfolio	See Chapter 13	
Mutual fund	See Chapter 13	
Cash	Current cash on hand	Today's date

To edit or hide an account:

1. Choose Lists > Accounts, or press Command-A. If it is not already open, the Accounts window appears (**Figure 2.8**).

2. Select an account and click the Edit button. The Edit Account window (which looks just like the Set Up Account window) appears.

3. Change the account information, and then click the Change button.

   Or

   If you no longer use an account and you don't want it cluttering up your Accounts window, you can hide it by clicking the "Hide in lists" check box in the Edit Account window. Then click the Change button.

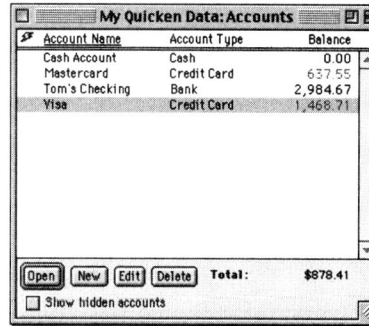

To delete an account:

1. Choose Lists > Accounts, or press Command-A. The Accounts window appears.

2. Select an account, and then click the Delete button. Click the Yes button when Quicken asks you to confirm the account deletion.

✔ Tips

■ You'll hardly ever need to delete an account. When you do, you lose the record of all the transactions that ever occurred in that account. Because this can mess up your reports, you're usually better off to hide an account.

■ If you ever need to see accounts that you've hidden, click the "Show hidden accounts" checkbox at the bottom of the Accounts window (refer to **Figure 2.8**).

Figure 2.8 You can hide, edit, or delete an account from the Accounts window.

Tracking
with Categories

The point of using Quicken is to gain better control over your finances. And to achieve that control, you'll need to know where your money comes from and where your money goes. You use Quicken's *categories* to track the flow of money. A category is simply a label that you assign to a transaction. For example, when you buy food at the grocery store and record the transaction in a Quicken register, you can record it under the category "Groceries." Later, when you're curious about how much money you spend on groceries, you can create a report that adds up all of your transactions for groceries.

By categorizing all of your transactions in Quicken, you can generate reports about the details of your income and expenses, save time and money while preparing your tax returns, and even set up budgets and compare what you're actually spending to what you had planned to spend.

Assigning Categories

Because categories are used to track the flow of money, you are naturally concerned about whether the money is flowing in or out. Money that is flowing in, such as your paycheck and investment income, are tracked using income categories. Money that you spend on your mortgage, utilities, groceries, entertainment, and other bills are tracked using expense categories.

You can—and should—assign a category to each transaction that you enter into Quicken. You should also use the same category names consistently throughout your Quicken accounts. For example, if you go to the doctor and pay with a check, you would enter that check under the "Medical" category in your checking account register. If on a subsequent visit you pay with a credit card, you would enter the transaction in your credit card account register using the category "Medical" This consistency is important: consistent data leads to accurate reports.

✔ Tip

- When you created your data file (see Chapter 2), you probably included one of the preset categories lists, either the home categories or the business categories. You can use these category lists as is, but most people end up customizing their categories to better reflect their particular financial situations.

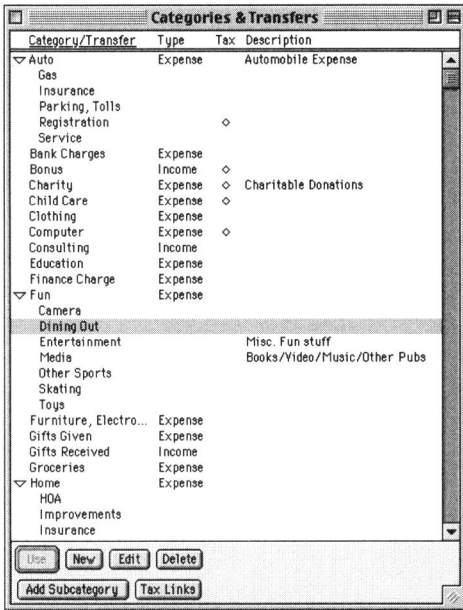

Figure 3.1 Click the New button in the Categories & Transfers window to create a new category.

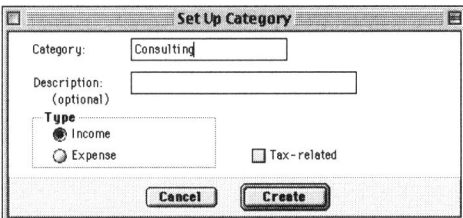

Figure 3.2 Enter a name and description in the Set Up Category dialog box.

To create a new category:

1. Choose Lists > Categories & Transfers, or press Command-L. The Categories & Transfers window appears (**Figure 3.1**).

2. At the bottom of the Categories & Transfers window, click the New button. The Set Up Category dialog box appears (**Figure 3.2**).

3. Enter a name for the category in the Category box.

4. Enter a description for the category in the Description box (optional).

5. Select the appropriate radio button for the new category type (Income or Expense).

6. Click the "Tax-related" check box if you want to use the category to track tax-related income or expenses.

7. Click the Create button. Quicken creates the category and adds it to the list in the Categories & Transfers window.

CREATING A NEW CATEGORY

Assigning Subcategories

You'll often want to track several types of income or expenses that are related to a single category. Quicken allows you to use subcategories to handle these relations. For example, under the Medical category, you might have separate subcategories for Doctors, Dentists, Prescriptions, and Insurance. Later, when you run an expense report, you'll be able to see just how much money you've spent on each of the Medical subcategories.

To create a subcategory:

1. In the Categories & Transfers window, select a category for which you would like to create a subcategory.

2. Click the Add Subcategory button. The Set Up Category dialog box appears, but the Type radio buttons are dimmed (**Figure 3.3**). That's because a subcategory must always be of the same type as its parent category.

3. Enter the subcategory name in the Category box.

4. Enter the subcategory description in the Description box (optional).

5. If necessary, click the "Tax-related" check box.

6. Click the Create button. Quicken creates the subcategory, indenting it under the main category in the Categories & Transfers window (Figure 3.4).

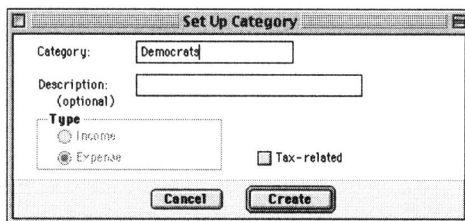

Figure 3.3 Enter the subcategory name and description in this dialog box.

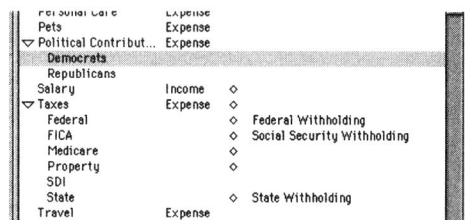

Figure 3.4 After you create a subcategory, Quicken adds its name to the Categories & Transfers window.

How Detailed Should I Get?

Quicken's preset categories are useful, but they're unlikely to completely satisfy your needs. No problem; just add more categories. But how much is enough?

The answer depends on the complexity of your financial picture and the level of detail to which you wish to track it. Here's an example. Robert is a salesman for a company and is constantly on the road. The company reimburses Robert for some of his auto expenses, so he tracks those expenses in great detail. Under his main Auto category, he has included subcategories for Maintenance, Fuel, Insurance, etc. Robert creates monthly Auto expense reports so that he can be reimbursed.

Susan works as an executive for the same corporation. She's curious to know how much she spends each year on her car. She doesn't care about the details; she just wants to know if her car expenses are growing or shrinking from year to year. So she uses one Auto category to track all expenses related to her car.

Your answer to the above question, then, depends on what kind of information is important to you. In general, you'll want to create subcategories for important elements so that you can track income or expenses in detail.

To edit or delete a category or subcategory:

1. Select the category or subcategory in the Categories & Transfers window.

2. Click the Edit button. The Edit Category window appears, which works in exactly the same way as the Set Up Category window. Make your changes, and then click the Change button.

   Or

   Click the Delete button. When Quicken asks you to confirm the deletion, click the Yes button.

EDIT OR DELETE A CATEGORY

Using Tax Links

Quicken makes it easy for you to create tax reports by marking a selected category as tax-related and then assigning that category to a line item from a particular tax form. Several of the preset categories are already assigned to tax forms; these are marked with a diamond character in the Categories & Transfers window.

To assign a tax link:

1. Select a category or subcategory in the Categories & Transfers window.

2. Click the Tax Links button. The Assign Tax Links window appears (**Figure 3.5**).

3. Scroll through the Line Item list, and select the appropriate line item. Click the Assign button.

4. Click the Done button. Quicken links that line item to the category you selected in step 1.

✔ Tip

- Tax Links are tied to individual lines (by description, not by line number) on the various federal tax forms. These lines sometimes change from year to year as the tax laws (and therefore forms) change. Quicken 98 is based on the 1997 tax year, so you should review your Tax Schedule report (see Chapter 16) to make sure that Quicken is categorizing Tax Links correctly for the 1998 and later tax years.

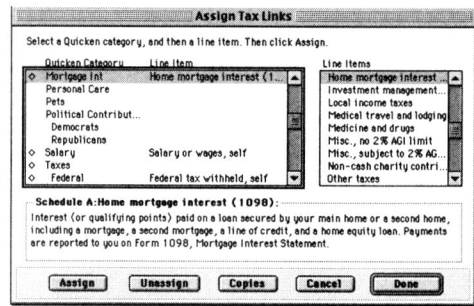

Figure 3.5 Select the appropriate line item from the list to assign the item to a category.

Figure 3.6 Click the New button in the Classes window to create a new class.

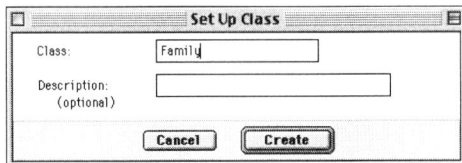

Figure 3.7 Enter the name and description of the new class here.

Using Classes

Classes are another way to group transactions. Classes do not replace categories; instead, a class adds an extra level to a transaction that has already been assigned to a category. When you assign a category to a transaction, you can also assign a class to the transaction by adding a slash (/) followed by the class name to the end of the category name. For example, Bob's medical expenses could be categorized as Medical/Bob.

You can use classes to avoid creating unnecessary subcategories. In the example above, it's possible (although inefficient) to add a Bob subcategory, another for Lisa, and so on for the entire family, all under the Medical category. The trouble with this is that you would need to create such subcategories for every category that could be assigned to a different family member. Pretty soon, you'd have about a zillion categories and subcategories. Instead, it's better to create a class for each family member and then assign that class to transactions as necessary.

Unlike categories, preset classes don't come with Quicken; you'll have to create and define your own. But like subcategories, subclasses are easy to create.

To create a class or subclass:

1. Choose Lists > Classes, or press Command-K. The Classes window appears (**Figure 3.6**).

2. Click the New button. The Set Up Class window appears (**Figure 3.7**). If you're creating a subclass, select the parent class, then click the Add Subclass button.

3. Enter the name and (optionally) the description of the class, and then click the Create button. The name of the new class appears in the Classes window.

To edit or delete a class or subclass:

1. Select the category or subcategory in the Classes window.

2. Click the Edit button. The Edit Class window appears, which works in the same way as the Set Up Class window. Make your changes, and then click the Change button.

   Or

   Click the Delete button. When Quicken asks you to confirm the deletion, click the Yes button.

✔ Tips

- Classes are a great way to differentiate personal and business expenses. For example, you can create a class called Business and assign it to categories that you also use for personal expenses. (For example, you can classify some meals as Dining/Business.)

- If you have many clients, you can use classes to track income expenses for each client separately. In the same way, you can create classes for projects or particular jobs.

- You can't change a class into a category or vice versa.

- If you rename a class, category, subclass, or subcategory, Quicken replaces the old name with the new one in all transactions that contained the old name.

- The items in the Categories & Transfers window and Classes window can be moved in the list by dragging them up or down. In this way, it's easy to demote a category to a subcategory or a class to a subclass, or vice versa.

EDIT OR DELETE A CLASS

USING THE
ACCOUNT REGISTERS

A *transaction* can be anything that changes the balance of an account. For a checking account, it could be writing a check, making a deposit, or withdrawing cash from the ATM. For a credit card account, it could be making a payment or a purchase. And for a stock portfolio account, transactions include buying shares and reinvesting dividends.

Every account in Quicken has an *account register* in which you enter transactions. Quicken's registers look and act much like paper check-book registers, which makes them familiar and easy to use. One nice difference from paper, however, is that a Quicken register does the math for you and keeps a running balance automatically.

In this chapter, you'll learn how to enter transactions in the account registers, how to enter your paycheck into Quicken, how to use Quicken to keep track of your credit cards, and how to use Quicken's data entry aids to save you typing and time.

Entering Checking Account Transactions

Checks, deposits, and transfers are all transactions that need to be entered in your account register. A checking account register (**Figure 4.1**) contains all the information (in boxes called fields) you need about a transaction, including date, check number, payee, payment or deposit amount, category, memo field, and check box to indicate whether the transaction has cleared your bank.

Checks that you intend to print from within Quicken can be entered either in the register or in the Write Checks window. (See Chapter 6 for more about printing checks.)

You enter information in a register by typing in a field and then pressing the Tab key to move to the next field.

To enter a check or a deposit:

1. Click the Banking button in the activity bar (**Figure 4.2**) to switch to Quicken's banking area.

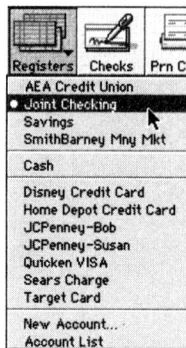

2. Click the Registers button in the task bar, and then choose a checking account from the pop-up menu (**Figure 4.3**).

3. The checking account register opens (refer to **Figure 4.1**) with the current date filled in and the Date field highlighted. You can change the date by typing in a new date, clicking the calendar icon underneath the date (**Figure 4.4**), or by using the date keyboard shortcuts shown in Table 4.1.

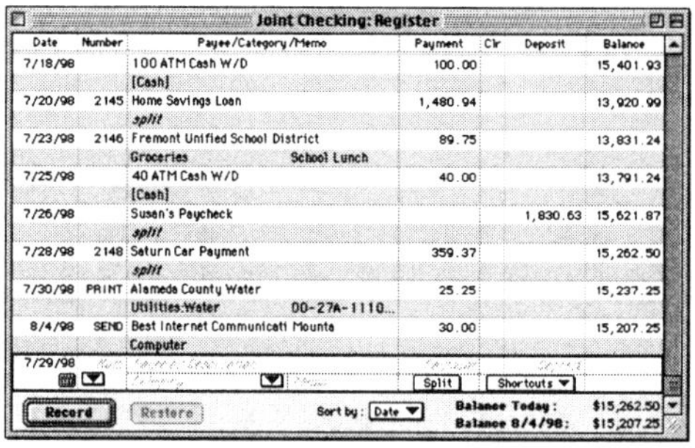

Figure 4.1 Enter transaction information in boxes called fields in the account register

Figure 4.2 Click the Banking button in the activity bar to switch to Quicken's banking area.

Figure 4.3 Choose a checking account from the pop-up menu.

Figure 4.4 Click the calendar icon to change the date.

Table 4.1

Keyboard shortcuts for the Date field

SHORTCUT	WHAT IT DOES
+	Next day
-	Previous day
t	Today
m	Beginning of the current month
h	End of the current month
y	Beginning of the current year
r	End of the current year
[	Same date last month
]	Same date next month
{	Same date last year
}	Same date next year

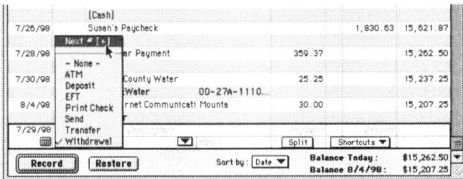

Figure 4.5 Choose a transaction type from the pop-up menu in the Number field.

4. Press the Tab key to move to the Number field (and see the Tip below).

5. If you're writing a check, enter the next check number in the Number field. To have Quicken automatically enter the next number in your check sequence, press the + key. If you're entering another kind of transaction, choose that transaction type from the pop-up menu in the Number field (**Figure 4.5**). See Table 4.2 for the keyboard shortcuts you can use for transaction types.

6. Enter the payee (for a check) or a description (for a deposit or transfer).

7. Enter the payment or deposit amount.

8. Assign a category to the transaction by typing it into the Category field. The QuickFill feature fills in the category name after you enter the first few letters. (See Chapter 5 for more information about QuickFill.) You can also use the pop-up menu in the Category field to select the category. If you want to add a class to the category, type a slash (/) at the end of the category name, and then type the class name (optional).

9. Enter a memo about the transaction (optional).

10. Click the Record button. Quicken saves the transaction and adds it to the register.

✔ Tips

- Press Tab whenever you need to move from one field to another in a register or dialog box.

- To use the Return key instead of the Tab key to move from field to field, choose Edit > Preferences and then click the Register icon in the left side of the window. Click the check box next to "Pressing Return tabs to the next field."

- If you need to write a post-dated check, simply enter a future date in the Date field. At the bottom of the register, Quicken will display the "Balance Today" and a future balance showing the balance as of the date of the post-dated check.

- To quickly enter a date in the current month, type the day in the Date field and press the Tab key. Quicken automatically enters the current month and year.

- You can't put a value in the Balance column because Quicken does the math for you.

- You can enter ATM withdrawals quickly by using QuickFill and starting your description with a number. For example, if you regularly withdraw $80, use the description 80 ATM. The next time you record an ATM withdrawal, simply type 80 and Quicken will automatically enter the correct amount.

- In any field that QuickFill works, you can use the up and down arrow keys to scroll alphabetically through the possible matches. For example, if you type Ho in the Description field, QuickFill might guess "Home Depot." Pressing the down arrow key would tell QuickFill to try the next possibility in the QuickFill list, "Home Savings." Pressing the up arrow key scrolls backwards alphabetically.

Table 4.2

Keyboard shortcuts for the Number field	
SHORTCUT	WHAT IT DOES
+	Enters the next check number
-	Subtracts a check number
a	ATM, an ATM transaction
d	DEP, a deposit
e	EFT, Electronic Funds Transfer
p	PRINT, a check to be printed
s	SEND, an electronic payment to be sent
t	TRANS, a transfer to another Quicken account
x	XFR, a transfer to another Quicken account (old, but still works)
w	WITHD, a cash withdrawal

Category pop-up menu

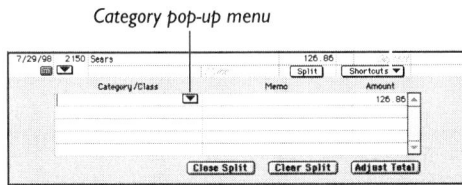

Figure 4.6 Use split lines to indicate separate payment categories in the register.

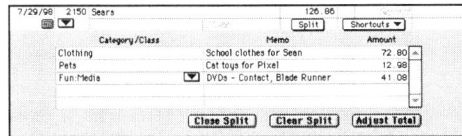

Figure 4.7 Enter category and amount information until you have allocated the entire payment or deposit amount.

Splitting Transactions

Many transactions need to be divided among multiple categories, referred to as *splitting* the transaction. For example, you might write a single check at a service station that covers both gasoline and auto repairs. When you enter that transaction, you will enter a category name and amount for each part of the split. You can split checks that you write or payments that you receive.

To split a transaction:

1. Open a checking account register.

2. Enter the date, check number, payee, and the payment or deposit amount.

3. Click the Split button and choose Edit > Split Transaction, or press Command-E. The split lines (where you enter additional categories and amounts) appear in the register (**Figure 4.6**).

4. Enter the category in the first Category field in the split, either by typing it in or by choosing it from the pop-up menu.

5. Type a memo in the first Memo field (optional).

6. Type the amount you want to allocate to the first category in the first Amount field. Quicken subtracts that amount from the total and puts the remainder in the next Amount field.

7. Enter the next category and amount on the next line. Repeat this until you have allocated the entire payment or deposit amount (**Figure 4.7**).

8. Click the Record button. The transaction is saved, properly allocated to multiple categories.

SPLITTING TRANSACTIONS

✔ Tips

■ If you decide that you don't want to split the transaction, click the Clear Split button, which deletes all the information in the split lines.

■ If you want to split amounts but don't want to figure the total amount by adding up the split amounts yourself, Quicken adds up the total for you. For example, if you make one deposit that includes several checks from different categories, enter the amounts in all the split lines. As you add information, Quicken updates the total amount in the Deposit field.

■ You can keep QuickFill from filling in splits by pressing Option-Tab to exit the Payee field. Quicken clears all of the QuickFill information except for the payee name.

■ You can add as many lines of categories as you need to a split transaction.

7/26/98	▼	Susan's Paycheck			1,830.63	15,621.87	
				Split	Shortcuts ▼		
		Category /Class	Memo		Amount		
		Salary	▼		2,738.47		
		Taxes:Federal			-358.59		
		Taxes:FICA			-154.85		
		Taxes:Medicare			-36.22		
		Taxes:State			-89.16		
		Taxes:SDI			-19.98		
		Medical:Premiums			-29.00		
		[Flex Health]			-12.00		
		[Flex Day Care]			-200.00		
		LTD			-2.64		
		Life Insurance			-5.40		

Figure 4.8 Enter your deductions as negative amounts so they will be subtracted from the gross amount.

Entering Paychecks

You enter paychecks as a split transaction, but with a bit of a difference: because paychecks are subject to payroll deductions, you need to show the gross amount and the deductions in the split lines.

To enter a paycheck:

1. Open a checking account register.

2. Enter the date, press the D key to add *DEP* to the Number field, enter a description, and then enter the net amount of your paycheck in the Deposit field. The net is your salary minus all the deductions: in other words, the amount of the check.

3. Click the Split button to open the split lines.

4. In the first Category field, enter *Salary*.

5. Enter a memo in the Memo field (optional).

6. Enter the gross amount of your salary in the first Amount field.

7. In the next Category field, enter the first category for your deductions. For example, you might want to use *Taxes:Federal* as the category.

8. In this and all subsequent split lines, enter your deductions as negative amounts so they will be subtracted from the gross (**Figure 4.8**). Keep adding lines until all your deductions are allocated.

9. Click the Record button.

✔ Tip

- Most people's paychecks don't change very often. You can save a lot of repetitive data entry by selecting the transaction and choosing Edit > Memorize Transaction, or pressing Command-M to memorize the amount.

ENTERING PAYCHECKS

Entering Credit Card Charges

Entering transactions in a credit card register is a lot like using a bank account register except that the headings Charge and Payment appear rather than Payment and Deposit (**Figure 4.9**). Another difference is that in a credit card register, you prefer a zero balance, something most people wouldn't want to see in their checking account.

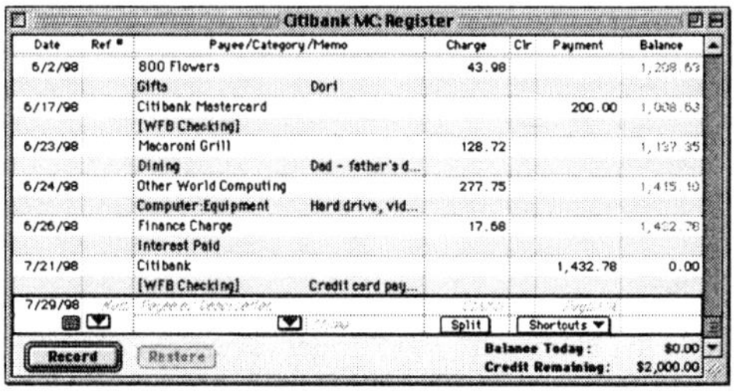

Figure 4.9 Enter information in the Charge and Payment fields in the credit card register.

To enter credit card charges:

1. Click the Banking button in the activity bar to open Quicken's banking area.

2. Click the Registers button in the task bar, and then choose a credit card account from the pop-up menu. The credit card's account register opens.

3. Enter the date of the credit card transaction.

   Notice that instead of the Check number field, there's an optional Reference number field.

1. Enter the payee and the amount of the charge.

2. Enter the category.

3. Enter a memo about the charge (optional).

4. Click the Record button.

✔ Tips

- You can dramatically reduce your data entry in credit card accounts by setting up the account for online banking, which lets you download all the transactions from the bank to the account register. See Chapter 9 for more information.

- Don't forget to enter finance charges.

ENTERING CREDIT CARD CHARGES

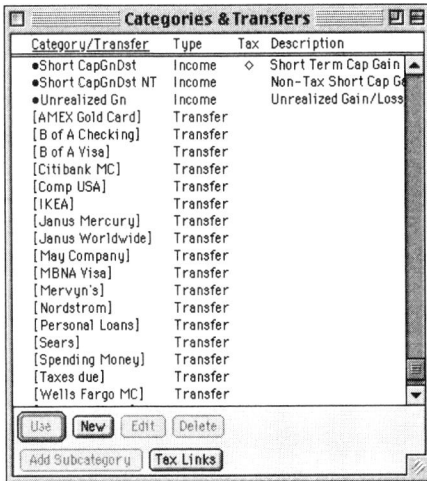

Figure 4.10 You can view the transfer categories in your data file by scrolling to the bottom of the Categories & Transfers window.

Transferring Money Between Accounts

Because you often need to transfer money between accounts, Quicken provides a way to perform this transaction. For example, when you write a check to make a payment to your credit card account, money flows out of the checking account and into the credit card account, decreasing the credit card's balance. Quicken makes it easy to update both accounts with one transaction so you don't have to enter the same transaction in both registers. To accomplish this, Quicken uses special categories called *transfer categories*, which refer to other Quicken accounts. You can view the transfer categories in your data file by choosing Lists > Categories & Transfers and scrolling to the bottom of the window (**Figure 4.10**).

In the first example below, you'll see how to use transfer categories to transfer money from your checking to your savings account. The next example shows you how to transfer money between accounts using the Transfer Money command.

To transfer money from one account to another:

1. Click the Banking button in the activity bar to open Quicken's banking area.

2. Click the Registers button in the task bar, and then choose a checking account from the pop-up menu. The checking account register appears.

3. Enter the date.

4. In the Number field, press the T key. Quicken will put *TRANS* in the number field to signify that this is a transfer.

5. Enter a description of the transfer in the Payee field.

6. In this example, money is moving from checking to savings, so enter an amount in the Payment field. (If the money were flowing from savings to checking, you would add the amount to the Deposit field.)

7. In the Category field, press the left bracket ([ ) key, and then type the name of the savings account.

Or

Choose the savings account from the pop-up menu in the Category field. Your register should look something like **Figure 4.11**.

8. Click the Record button. Quicken saves the transaction in the checking account register and creates a parallel transaction in the savings account register (**Figure 4.12**).

Figure 4.11 Click the Record button and Quicken saves the transaction.

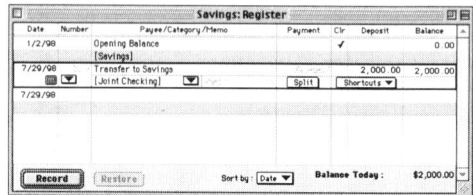

Figure 4.12 You can see a parallel transaction in the savings account register.

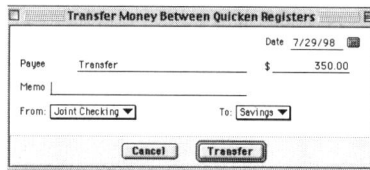

To use the Transfer Money command:

1. Choose Activities > Transfer Money. The Transfer Money Between Quicken Registers window appears (**Figure 4.13**).

2. Enter the date, a description in the Payee field (*Transfer* appears here by default), the amount you want to transfer, and a memo (optional).

3. Using the "From" pop-up menu, choose the source account for the transfer.

4. Using the "To" pop-up menu, choose the destination account for the transfer.

5. Click the Transfer button. Quicken creates a transaction in both the source and destination accounts.

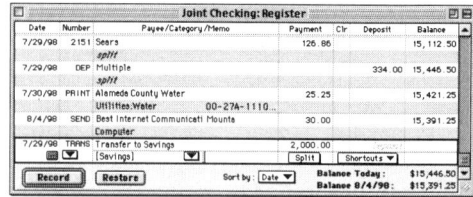

Figure 4.13 Enter transaction information in the Transfer Money Between Quicken Registers window.

Are you sure you want to delete?

No   Yes

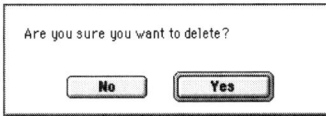

Figure 4.14 Click Yes to confirm the transaction deletion.

Changing Transactions

Unlike some other financial programs, Quicken allows you to make changes to transactions at any time. You can edit, delete, or void transactions whenever necessary.

To edit a transaction:

1. Open the account register that contains the transaction you want to edit.

2. Click on a transaction to select it.

3. In any field of the transaction, select the incorrect information and type over it to replace it.

4. Click the Record button.

To delete a transaction:

1. Open the account register that contains the transaction you want to delete.

2. Click on a transaction to select it.

3. Choose Edit > Delete Transaction, or press Command-D. Quicken will ask you to confirm the deletion (**Figure 4.14**).

4. Click the Yes button. Quicken deletes the transaction.

To void a transaction:

1. Open the account register that contains the transaction you want to void.

2. Click on a transaction to select it.

3. Choose Edit > Void Transaction. Quicken removes the amount in the Payment or Deposit field and places the word *VOID* at the beginning of the Payee field.

4. Click the Record button.

CHANGING TRANSACTIONS

To find a transaction:

You can search through account registers to find a particular transaction. This feature is most useful when you're entering a transaction and wish to be reminded of the details of a previous transaction.

1. Open the account register in which you want to find a transaction.

2. Choose Edit > Find/Replace > Find, or press Command-F. The Find dialog box will appear (**Figure 4.15**).

3. In the Find field, enter the text that you wish to search for. Make choices from the "Search" and "Match if" pop-up menus to narrow your search.

4. Click the Next button to find the next occurrence of your search text.

5. When you're done with your search, click the Close box in the Find window.

✔ Tip

- When you're looking for multiple transactions, you're better off switching to the Reports section and running a QuickReport. See Chapter 10 for more information about reports.

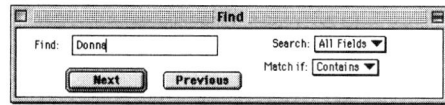

Figure 4.15 Enter the text that you wish to search for in the Find field.

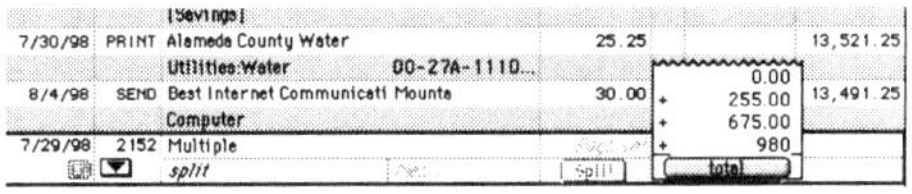

Figure 4.16 Enter the numbers you wish to calculate, pressing an operator key between each number.

Using Data Entry Helpers

Two other useful data entry tools you should know about are QuickMath and QuickEntry. QuickMath lets you make simple mathematical calculations right in the account register, and QuickEntry (found only in Quicken Deluxe) allows you to enter transactions without even opening Quicken.

QuickMath

QuickMath gives you a simple "paper tape" calculator right in the account register. If you want to make simple calculations while entering a transaction—for example adding up a bunch of checks while you're filling out the deposit transaction—QuickMath will make it easier.

To use QuickMath:

1. Begin entering a transaction in an account register.

2. For any field in which you can enter an amount, press an arithmetic operator key (+, -, *, /, or =) to pop up a "paper tape." You can enter numbers here as you would on an adding machine (**Figure 4.16**).

3. Enter the numbers you wish to calculate, pressing an operator key between each number. When you have entered all your numbers, click the "total" button at the bottom of the paper tape. Quicken does the calculation and places the result in the amount field.

QuickEntry

If you enter transactions every day (and even if you don't), QuickEntry can reduce the time it takes. QuickEntry is a small application that opens quickly and lets you enter data into all of your bank, credit card, and cash account registers. You enter transactions into QuickEntry in exactly the same way you would into Quicken. QuickEntry data is stored in your Quicken data file and added to your Quicken registers the next time you open the Quicken program.

To use QuickEntry:

1. Choose QuickEntry from the Apple menu. The QuickEntry window appears (**Figure 4.17**).

2. Choose the account to which you want to enter data from the Account pop-up menu. After you make the change, the Ending Balance for that account is displayed in QuickEntry's lower right corner.

3. Enter transactions as you would in any Quicken register, clicking the Record button after each entry.

4. When you're done making entries, choose File > Quit.

5. The next time you open your Quicken data file, the QuickEntry Transactions window will appear (**Figure 4.18**), recapping the entries you made in QuickEntry. Click the OK button and Quicken adds the QuickEntry transactions to your registers and removes those entries from QuickEntry.

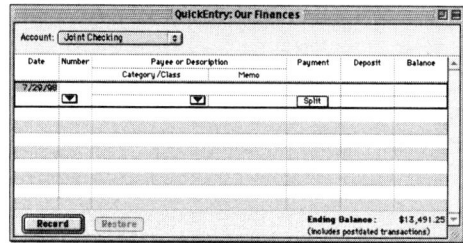

Figure 4.17 Choose QuickEntry from the Apple menu to open the QuickEntry window.

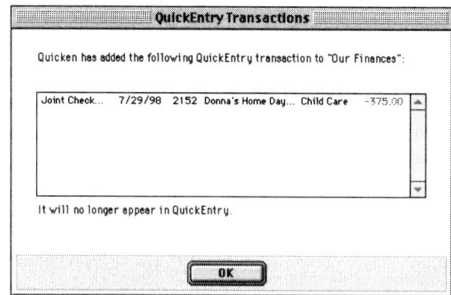

Figure 4.18 Click the OK button and Quicken will add the QuickEntry transactions to your registers.

5

ALL ABOUT QUICKFILL

If your financial situation is anything like mine, you find yourself repeating similar transactions over and over. For example, you probably make a rent or mortgage payment every month and deposit your paycheck biweekly or once a month. You probably also pay many of the same bills every month—to the phone company, to your electric utility, to your supermarket for groceries, whatever. You could simply type in all of that stuff again and again and again, but why bother? That's the kind of repetitive dog work for which computers were designed. You can let your computer remember and enter the boring stuff by using the QuickFill feature in Quicken.

QuickFill watches over your shoulder as you type information into an account register or onto a check. When the information you're typing matches a previous transaction, QuickFill enters the rest of the transaction for you. QuickFill can remember all or part of a transaction, so you can use it to remember and enter transactions whose amounts stay the same every month (such as your rent or mortgage payment) or transactions that can change each month (like the electric bill).

In this chapter, you'll learn how to use QuickFill to make entering transactions easier and to memorize, edit, enter, and delete QuickFill transactions.

How QuickFill Works

Let's face it—there's nothing especially fun or glamorous about entering your transactions into an account register. In fact, it can be downright dull. QuickFill is an important tool that helps you get information into Quicken fast and with less boredom.

Every time you enter a transaction in your account register or on a check, Quicken adds the information to the QuickFill Transaction list. Then, when you create a new entry, Quicken compares the information in the QuickFill list to what you're typing. As soon as it finds a match, QuickFill fills in the rest of the transaction for you. If QuickFill's guess is correct, all you'll probably need to do is change the amount of that particular check. If QuickFill guesses wrong, you keep typing and your entry will replace QuickFill's guess.

You can also manually add transactions to QuickFill's list by selecting a transaction and manually "memorizing" it. You can view, use, edit, or delete QuickFill transactions via the QuickFill Transactions window (**Figure 5.1**).

✔ Tips

- Keep in mind that Quicken won't add information to the QuickFill list from the account registers in the Investment section.

- You can turn QuickFill on or off, and you can turn off the automatic updating of the QuickFill list. To do so, choose Edit > Preferences to open the Preferences window. Click the Register icon. Then click on or off the check boxes next to "Use QuickFill to fill in transactions" and "Add new transactions to the QuickFill list." (**Figure 5.2**)

Figure 5.1 The QuickFill Transactions list helps you save a tremendous amount of time and keystrokes.

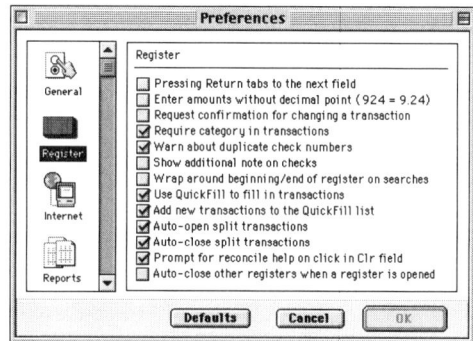

Figure 5.2 You can turn QuickFill on or off in the Register Preferences window.

Locked transactions

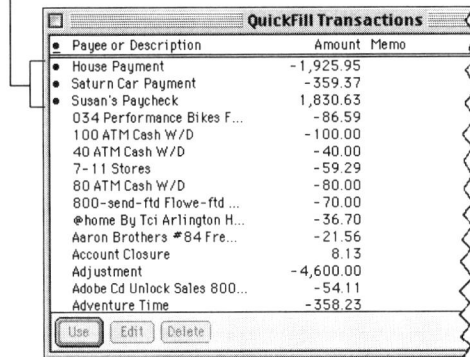

QuickFill Transactions		
Payee or Description	Amount	Memo
• House Payment	-1,925.95	
• Saturn Car Payment	-359.37	
• Susan's Paycheck	1,830.63	
034 Performance Bikes F...	-86.59	
100 ATM Cash W/D	-100.00	
40 ATM Cash W/D	-40.00	
7-11 Stores	-59.29	
80 ATM Cash W/D	-80.00	
800-send-ftd Flowe-ftd ...	-70.00	
@home By Tci Arlington H...	-36.70	
Aaron Brothers #84 Fre...	-21.56	
Account Closure	8.13	
Adjustment	-4,600.00	
Adobe Cd Unlock Sales 800...	-54.11	
Adventure Time	-358.23	

[Use] [Edit] [Delete]

Figure 5.3 Quicken indicates locked transactions by adding a black dot to the left of the transaction in the QuickFill list.

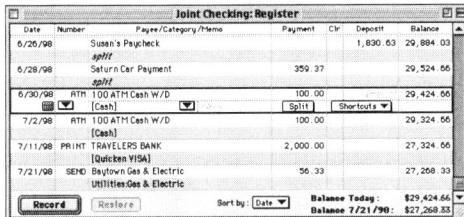

Joint Checking: Register							
Date	Number	Payee/Category/Memo	Payment	Clr	Deposit	Balance	
6/26/98		Susan's Paycheck			1,830.63	29,884.03	
		split					
6/28/98		Saturn Car Payment	359.37			29,524.66	
		split					
6/30/98		ATM 100 ATM Cash W/D	100.00			29,424.66	
		[Cash]			Split	Shortcuts ▼	
7/2/98		ATM 100 ATM Cash W/D	100.00			29,324.66	
		[Cash]					
7/11/98	PRINT	TRAVELERS BANK	2,000.00			27,324.66	
		[Quicken VISA]					
7/21/98	SEND	Baytown Gas & Electric	56.33			27,268.33	
		Utilities:Gas & Electric					

[Record] [Restore] Sort by: [Date ▼] Balance Today: $29,424.66
Balance 7/21/98: $27,268.33

Figure 5.4 Quicken indicates which transaction is selected in a register by adding a border around it.

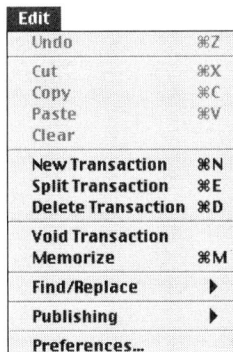

Edit	
Undo	⌘Z
Cut	⌘X
Copy	⌘C
Paste	⌘V
Clear	
New Transaction	⌘N
Split Transaction	⌘E
Delete Transaction	⌘D
Void Transaction	
Memorize	⌘M
Find/Replace	▶
Publishing	▶
Preferences...	

Figure 5.5 Choose Memorize from the Edit menu, or press Command+M.

Memorizing Transactions

Usually you won't need to do anything to memorize a transaction and add it to the QuickFill Transactions list. Quicken will do it for you automatically. See for yourself: you have already entered some data into Quicken, open the QuickFill Transactions list by choosing Lists > QuickFill Transactions to see the automatically memorized transactions.

Sometimes, however, you'll want to manually memorize a transaction, usually because you want to lock or unlock it. The black dots that appear at the left of the transactions in **Figure 5.3** indicate locked transactions. You can unlock transactions so that QuickFill will memorize any changes, or you can lock them so that the QuickFill entry will not update should you make any changes to the register entry.

Unlocked transactions are typically used for transactions that are written to the same payee but with different details. For example, you might often write checks out to Safeway, but the amount and even the category might vary with every check.

Locked QuickFill transactions are useful for checks written to the same payee for which the details rarely change, such as a car payment. You can still change the amount in the register or on the check, but that won't affect the memorized amount stored in a locked QuickFill transaction.

To manually memorize a QuickFill transaction:

1. In your account register, select a transaction by clicking it. Quicken adds a border around the transaction you selected (**Figure 5.4**).

2. Choose Edit > Memorize, or press Command-M (**Figure 5.5**).

Using QuickFill Transactions

QuickFill usually works unobtrusively, automatically popping in information as you enter transactions in account registers or on checks. But you can also use the QuickFill Transactions list manually to help you add transactions by keeping the QuickFill Transactions list open while entering data.

Why would you want to do this? Here's one example. I use three telephone lines in my house, one personal, the other two business related, so I track expenditures on all three separately. Naturally, the lines are all maintained by the same phone company so the payee is the same. If I used QuickFill in the usual fashion, I couldn't track which QuickFill transactions cover the personal line and which ones cover the business lines. So I open the QuickFill Transactions window, where each transaction includes a Memo field indicating the type of phone line to which the transaction applies.

To use the QuickFill Transactions list to help enter transactions:

1. With your account register open, choose Lists > QuickFill Transactions. The QuickFill Transactions window opens (**Figure 5.6**).

2. Scroll through the QuickFill Transactions list until you find the transaction that you want to use.

3. Click on the transaction to highlight it.

4. Click the Use button to transfer the contents of the transaction to the open account register. Or, drag a transaction from the QuickFill Transactions window and drop it on the account register. Or, even simpler, double-clicking the transaction also enters it in the account register.

Figure 5.6 You can enter QuickFill transactions manually.

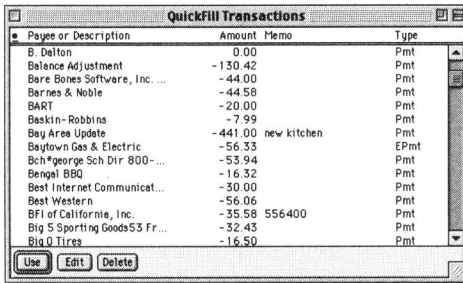

Figure 5.7 Open the QuickFill Transactions window to make changes to an individual transaction.

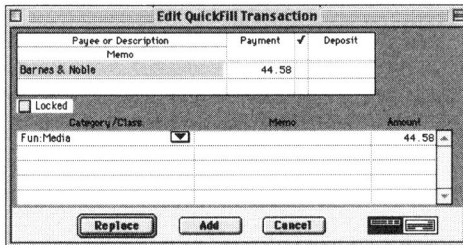

Figure 5.8 You can edit a transaction in the Edit QuickFill Transaction window.

Editing QuickFill Transactions

You can change any part of a QuickFill transaction, although you won't usually need to. Most often, you'll clear the amount of a transaction and then lock the transaction so that in future transactions with the same payee, you'll simply fill in the amount of the check.

To edit a QuickFill transaction:

1. Choose Lists > QuickFill Transactions. The QuickFill Transactions window appears (**Figure 5.7**).

2. Click once on the transaction that you want to edit to select it.

3. Click the Edit button at the bottom of the QuickFill Transaction window. The Edit QuickFill Transaction window appears (**Figure 5.8**).

4. Make any needed changes in the Payee or Description, Payment, Category/Class, Memo, or Amount fields. Notice that you can use split transactions (see Chapter 4).

5. To replace the transaction with your changes, click the Replace button. Or, to create a new QuickFill transaction with the edited information, click the Add button. Or, to back out of the window without saving changes, click the Cancel button.

To lock or unlock a QuickFill transaction:

1. Follow steps 1 through 4 above.

2. To lock a transaction, click the "Locked" check box in the Edit QuickFill Transaction window. To unlock the transaction, clear the "Locked" check box.

3. The QuickFill Transactions list indicates locked transactions by adding a black dot next to them (refer to **Figure 5.3**).

Deleting QuickFill Transactions

You might choose to get rid of a QuickFill transaction because it lists a payee that you dealt with only once, or to eliminate duplicate entries.

To delete a QuickFill transaction:

1. In the QuickFill Transactions window, click once on the transaction that you want to eliminate. Quicken highlights the memorized transaction.

2. Click the Delete button at the bottom of the QuickFill Transactions window.

✔ Tips

- If you leave a QuickFill transaction unlocked, Quicken replaces the amount of the check in the transaction every time you use the QuickFill entry. The next time you use that QuickFill entry, you'll see the amount of the last check you wrote to that payee. This makes it easy to tell if your spending with that payee has changed drastically. If it has, you have a chance to either rethink your spending pattern or check for an error in the current month's bill. I once found a $75 error in a utility bill in this fashion.

- If a loan transaction is listed in your QuickFill Transactions list, you won't be able to edit it from the QuickFill Transactions window. You'll need to go to the Loans window (choose Lists > Loans). For more about changing loan information, see Chapter 12.

Writing and Printing Checks

Just to avoid any possible confusion, this chapter is about writing checks that you intend to print from Quicken, on preprinted check forms. Checks that you write by hand should be entered into Quicken in your checking account register, as shown in Chapter 4.

If you don't already use Quicken to print your checks on preprinted check forms, you should definitely reconsider. When I was researching this book, I discovered that a surprising number of people don't use the program's printing abilities. If you're one of those folks, you're missing out on a lot of convenience. Consider: when you write checks by hand in your regular checkbook, you first fill out the check. Then you'll have to type all the same information into Quicken's check register. That's a lot of double work.

Using Quicken to print your checks can also help you avoid errors. Before I started printing checks, I'd discover (usually after chasing numbers for a good half hour when balancing my checkbook) that I had typed an incorrect amount for a handwritten check into the Quicken register. But when you write a check in Quicken in the first place, there's no chance of a pesky typo wasting your time later, because Quicken automatically enters each check amount into its register. It makes checkbook balancing much faster.

Ordering Checks

You can buy checks preprinted with your name, address, bank name and account number, check numbers, and any other information required by your bank. These checks are designed for use in laser printers and ink jet printers (you can also order continuous checks for dot-matrix printers), and they generally come in one of three styles:

- **Standard Checks** are sized for use in a business-size envelope and come three to a page (**Figure 6.7**).

- **Voucher Checks** are good for payroll and accounts payable use; you get one check per page, with two check stubs that you can keep or send out with the check as needed (**Figure 6.8**).

- **Wallet Checks** are smaller than standard checks (so that they can, not surprisingly, fit into your wallet) and include a stub for recording check information when writing a check by hand (**Figure 6.9**).

After you decide which style makes the most sense for you, have your current checkbook ready (you'll need it for the bank information and your account number) and order your checks. But where to get computer checks? One place is from Intuit itself, although they tend to charge more than some other companies. Many other business supply companies can provide checks and save you some money. See **Table 6.1** for some suggestions.

Figure 6.7 Standard checks are the ones used by most people, because they're the most convenient.

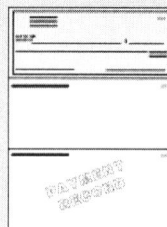

Figure 6.8 Voucher checks are good if you need a paper trail of check stubs. But for most of us, the less paper, the better.

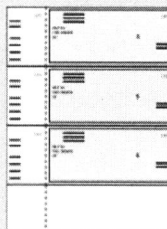

Figure 6.9 Wallet-style checks make sense if you want to carry your computer checks with you.

Table 6.1

Sources for Computer Checks

COMPANY	PHONE NUMBER	URL
Intuit	800-787-6748	www.intuitmarketplace.com
NEBS	800-225-6380	www.nebs.com
Checks for Less	800-325-5568	www.checksforless.com
PC Checks	800-322-5317	www.pcchecks.com
Sensible Solutions	888-852-4325	www.sensible-solutions.com

Figure 6.1 Click the Checks button in the task bar to open the Write Checks window.

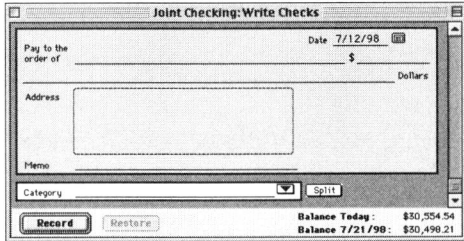

Figure 6.2 The Write Checks window looks like a real check, and you fill it out in much the same way that you fill out a regular check.

Calendar button

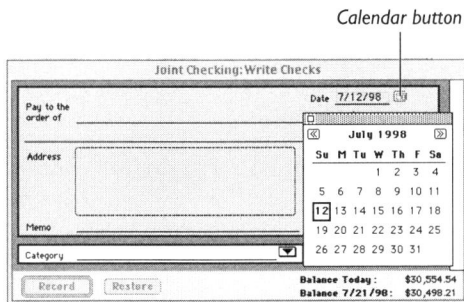

Figure 6.3 You can choose a date for the check from the calendar pop-up window.

To write a check:

1. Open the Write Checks window by choosing Activities > Write Checks, by pressing Command-J, or by clicking the Checks button on the task bar (**Figure 6.1**). The Write Checks window for your main checking account appears (**Figure 6.2**).

2. In the Write Checks window, today's date is entered for you and highlighted. If you want to change the date, type in a new date.

   or

   Click the Calendar button in the Write Checks window and a small calendar will pop up (**Figure 6.3**). Click on the new date in the small calendar window to add that date to the check.

3. Type in the name of the payee. As you type, QuickFill will anticipate and fill in the payee's name if what you're typing is similar to a name that appears on a previously written check. (See Chapter 5 for more about QuickFill.)

4. QuickFill fills in the same amount that appeared on the last check you wrote to that payee, which is handy for checks that you write each month for the same amount. Press the Tab key to move on if the amount is correct. If it's not correct, fill in the amount of the check.

   On the next line, Quicken turns the amount you entered into its text form. (For $42.76, for example, Quicken enters *Forty-two and 76/100*.)

5. Enter the name and address of the payee in the Address field (optional). To copy and paste the payee's name into the first line of the Address field, press the single quotation mark (') key.

WRITING CHECKS

6. Fill in the Memo field to record a memo about this check (optional).

7. If QuickFill entered the appropriate payee in step 3, it probably filled in the Category field correctly as well, and you can move on to the next step. Otherwise type in the appropriate category or use the Category pop-up menu to select one.

Click the Record button or press the Enter key. The completed check should look similar to that shown in **Figure 6.4**.

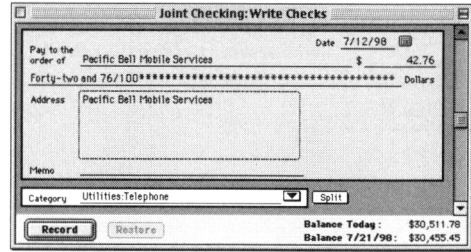

Figure 6.4 Your completed check should look something like this.

✔ Tips

■ The Write Checks window is usually the one for your main checking account (you can tell because the name of the account shows up in the title bar of the Write Checks window), but you can force it to appear for other accounts from which you can write checks. Just open the account's register for that account before you open the Write Checks window.

■ If you mail your printed checks in a windowed mailing envelope, the Memo line may be visible through the window. Adding confidential account numbers to the Memo line would be unsuitable. You can use another space to add these numbers. Choose Edit > Preferences, click the Register icon, and click "Show additional note on checks" (**Figure 6.5**). A note line will appear on the check (**Figure 6.6**). You can fill in this note line only from the Write Checks window; the account register doesn't show it. This note line also won't appear in the envelope window.

■ To memorize transactions in the Write Checks window as well as in the account register, choose Edit > Memorize or press Command-M.

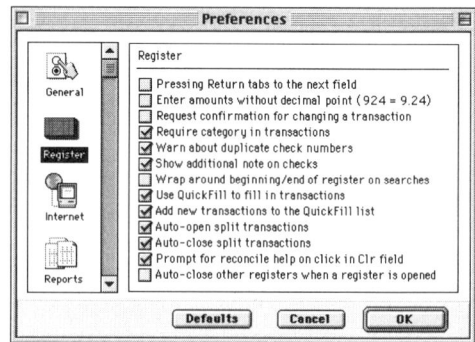

Figure 6.5 Use the Register section of Quicken's Preferences window to turn on a note field on checks.

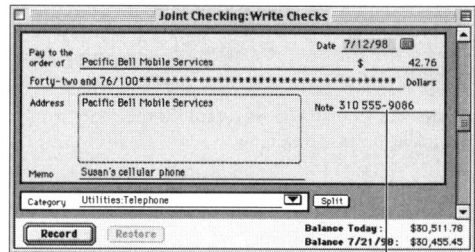

Note line

Figure 6.6 Type your account number on a check in the note line.

Writing Checks by Hand

When you're away from home, you can write checks with the checkbook that your bank provided when you opened your account, or you can use your preprinted computer checks and fill them out by hand. I like to use my regular bank checkbook and enter the information into Quicken when I return home. I differentiate between the checks that Quicken prints and ones I handwrite by using two widely different sets of check numbers for each kind of check. For example, I started my computer checks at 1000 and my handwritten checks start in the 4000 range. Quicken has no problem dealing with different sets of check numbers.

To edit a check:

1. Use the vertical scroll bar in the Write Checks window to scroll through checks you've written in the current session.

2. Find the check and edit the information.

3. Click the Record button or press the Enter key to save your work.

✔ Tip

■ If you prefer, you can edit the check by making changes in the account register. (See Chapter 4 for how to use the account register.) After you print a check, it disappears from the Write Checks window and is entered in the account register. Note that the check is accessible only from the account register after it has been printed.

To delete a check:

1. Scroll in the Write Checks window until you find the check you want to delete.

2. Choose Edit > Delete Transaction, or press Command-D. Quicken will pop up a dialog box asking you if you're sure you want to delete this check.

3. Click the Yes button to confirm the deletion.

✔ Tips

■ You can neither delete a check nor edit check information from the Write Checks window after the check has been printed. If you need to change or delete check information after you have printed a check, you can access the information from the account register. See Chapter 4 for more information.

■ Looking to void a check? You have to do that in the account register. See "Voiding Transactions" in Chapter 4 for more information.

Getting Ready to Print

After you have entered your checks for printing in the Write Checks window or in the account register, you're almost ready to print. But first you must set up Quicken to use your checks.

To set up Quicken to print:

1. From the Apple menu, select Chooser.

2. In the Chooser window (**Figure 6.10**), select the printer you want to use, and then close the window.

3. In Quicken, choose Edit > Preferences.

4. Click the Print Checks icon from the scrolling panel on the left (**Figure 6.11**).

5. Each bank account can have its own Print Checks settings. From the Account pop-up menu, choose the account to which you want these settings to apply.

6. Choose the font and font size you want printed on your checks.

7. Pick a style (standard, voucher, or wallet) from the Check Style pop-up menu.

8. Depending on how your particular printer feeds paper, choose one of the four alignments when printing one or two checks.

9. Unless you have a continuous-feed printer, leave the Sheet feeder check box checked.

10. If you're using voucher checks, check the "Print categories on voucher checks" check box.

11. Click the OK button to save your settings for this checking account.

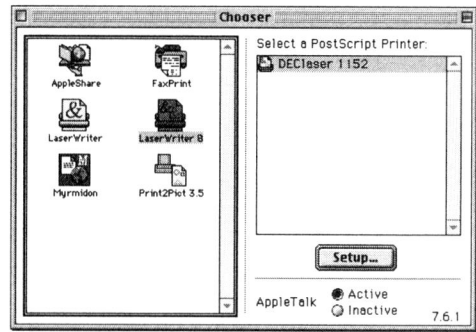

Figure 6.10 Select which printer you want to use from the Chooser window. For most printers, Quicken's default settings will do just fine.

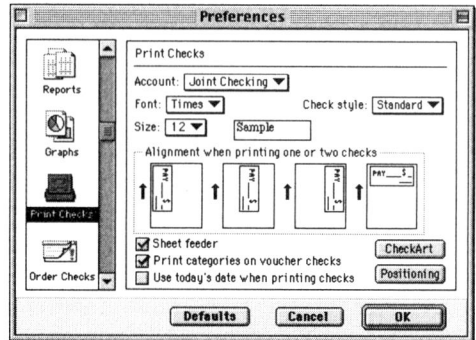

Figure 6.11 In the Print Checks Preferences window, you can create different check printing settings for each account. Clicking the CheckArt button allows you to print an image, such as a logo, on your checks.

Figure 6.12 Clicking the Print Checks button on the task bar is your entrée to check-printing bliss.

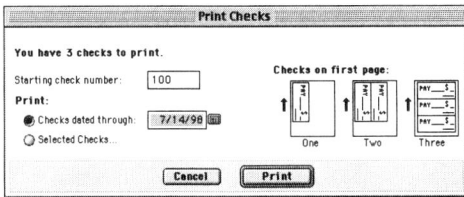

Figure 6.13 The Print Checks window tells you how many checks are set to print.

Printing Checks

Now that you've set up Quicken's printing functions, it's finally time to print. Note that most of the setup needs to be done only once; you'll just be printing merrily away.

To print checks:

1. Make sure the checks are in your printer tray and positioned correctly for printing. You might want to run a test on some plain paper before you print on real checks for the first time.

2. Verify that your printer is turned on and that it is online.

3. Open the account from which you want to print checks.

4. Choose File > Print Checks, or press Command-P, or click the Print Checks button from the task bar (**Figure 6.12**). The Print Checks window appears (**Figure 6.13**), telling you how many checks are ready to print.

5. The starting check number should match the first number of the checks that you put in the printer. If it doesn't match, change it. (In the future, Quicken will remember the number of the last check that you printed and automatically add the next number in this space.)

6. Add a date in the "Checks dated through" box to print all checks written up to this date. You'll probably use this option most often.

   or

   Click the Selected Checks radio button to open the Select Checks to Print dialog box (**Figure 6.14**). In the Print column, put a checkmark next to the checks that you want to print, and then click OK.

7. In the Print Checks window, click Print to open the printer dialog box.

8. Click the Print button in the printer dialog box to start printing checks.

9. After the checks have been printed, Quicken will ask you whether all the checks printed correctly (**Figure 6.15**). If they did, click Yes and Quicken will enter the check numbers into the account register.

If any of the checks did not print correctly (usually because of a printer problem), click No and Quicken will ask you to type in the number of the first incorrectly printed check. Fix the printer problem and start again at step 4 above to print the remaining checks.

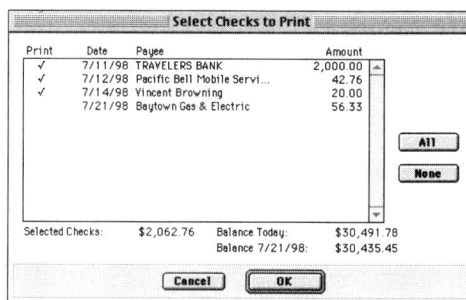

Figure 6.14 If you want to print particular checks, use the Select Checks to Print dialog box.

✔ Tips

■ To stop printing in the middle of a print job, press Command-. (period).

■ You can reprint a check at any time (if a payee loses a check, for example). Just replace the check number in your register with the word PRINT, and click the Record button. Then print the check normally.

■ Quicken's User Manual includes a chart showing Mac printers and how to position checks in their printer trays for correct printing. Refer to Chapter 7 of the manual for more information.

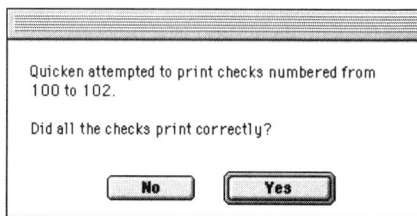

Figure 6.15 Quicken needs reassurance that your checks printed correctly. Soothe it by clicking the Yes button.

USING THE CALENDAR

When a bill gets paid is often as important as the amount of the payment. Because many of your financial transactions are time-sensitive, Quicken gives you a tool that lets you see your transactions over time: the Financial Calendar. With the Calendar, you can schedule future transactions and set up recurring transactions that need be paid on a regular schedule, such as mortgage payments or utility bills. Scheduled transactions can be entered automatically, saving you the drudgery of data entry. The Calendar can also remind you of upcoming payments and give you a quick visual overview of how you spend your money each month.

Working with the Calendar

To display the calendar, choose Activities > Calendar, or click the Calendar button in the task bar (**Figure 7.1**). The Financial Calendar will appear (**Figure 7.2**). The current day is automatically highlighted, and each financial transaction you've made in the current month is listed in black text on the day that it was created. Scheduled transactions that have not yet been paid are listed in blue text.

The controls at the top of the Financial Calendar let you change the month or year that is displayed. Controls at the bottom of the calendar let you view transactions for your accounts and enter new transactions.

To add a new transaction:

1. In the Calendar, select the date on which you wish to schedule a transaction.

2. At the bottom of the Calendar window, click the New Transaction button. The Enter Transaction window appears (**Figure 7.3**).

3. Using the buttons in the upper right corner of the Enter Transactions window, choose the mode in which you want to enter the transaction.

    By default, the Enter Transaction screen is set to account register mode, in which you can enter a transaction just as you enter a transaction into an account register. If you plan to create transactions that will be sent via online bill payment and have already enabled online bill payment (see Chapter 9), you can switch to that mode, as shown in **Figure 7.4**. Or you can enter calendar transactions in the familiar write checks mode, as shown in **Figure 7.5**.

4. Click on the down arrow in the Account area to see the Account pop-up menu.

Figure 7.1 Click the Calendar button to display the, well, calendar.

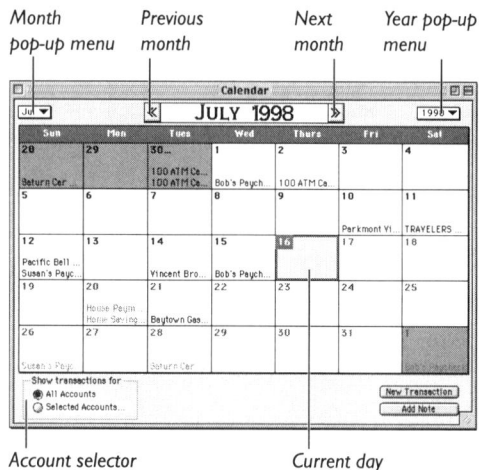

Figure 7.2 If you like, you can do all your data entry in the Financial Calendar.

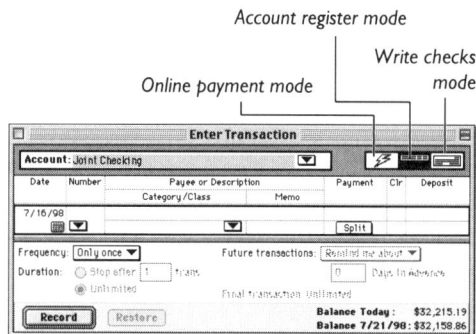

Figure 7.3 The Enter Transaction screen's default mode acts like an account register.

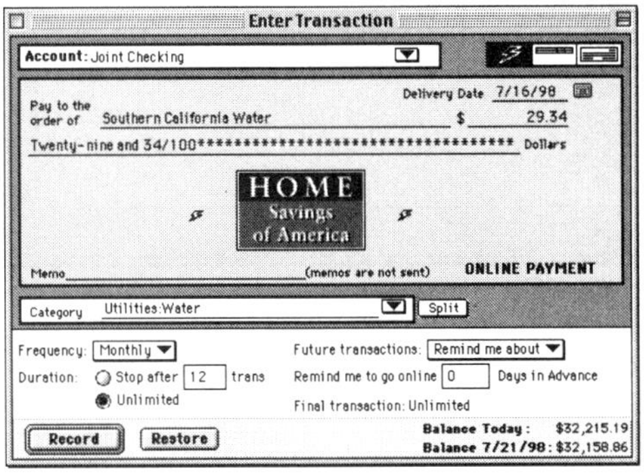

Figure 7.4 If you would rather pay your bills online, you can do so in the Enter Transaction window's online payment mode.

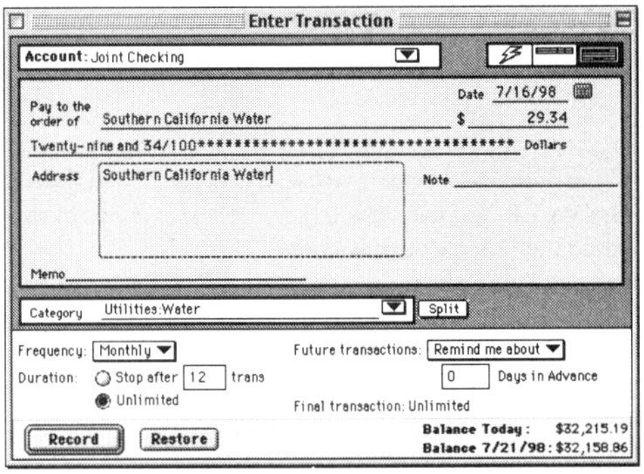

Figure 7.5 If you prefer printing checks, you can use write checks mode.

Figure 7.6 The Frequency pop-up menu allows you to select how often a transaction will recur.

Choose the account against which you'll apply the transaction.

5. By default, the current date appears in the Date field. You can leave this date as is or change it to another date.

6. In account register mode, with the cursor in the Number field, press the plus key [+] on your keyboard to enter the next check number. If you plan to print the check, you could also type PRINT in the Number field.

7. Enter the payee's name. As you're typing, QuickFill looks at names that you've entered previously in this area. If it finds a match, it adds the name. If this name is incorrect, you can simply change it.

8. In the Payment field, enter the amount.

9. Type in the category or click the down arrow in the Category area to select the category of the transaction.

10. Enter a memo about the transaction (optional).

11. If necessary, split the transaction (optional). See Chapter 4 for more about splitting transactions.

12. If this is a one-time transaction, leave Frequency set to "Only once." If this will be a recurring transaction, select how often it will recur from the Frequency pop-up menu (**Figure 7.6**).

13. In the Duration area, select either the "Un-limited" or the "Stop after [blank] trans-actions" radio button and fill in the blank.

14. In the Future transactions pop-up menu, choose either "Remind me about" or "Automatically enter." Whichever you choose, to enter the information in advance of the selected date, fill in the "Days in Advance" field with a number.

15. Click Record to save the transaction.

To edit a transaction:

1. In the Financial Calendar, double-click on the day that contains the transaction that you want to edit. The Transaction window for that day appears, as shown in **Figure 7.7**.

2. Double-click on the transaction that you want to edit. The Edit Transaction window, which looks and acts exactly like the Enter Transaction window, appears.

3. Make any changes you want, and then click the Record button.

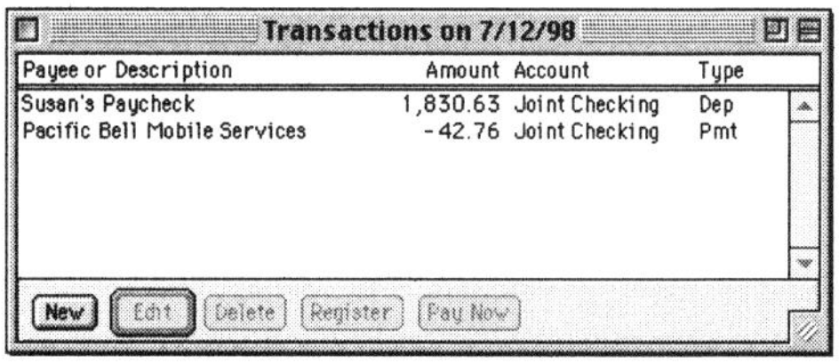

To view scheduled transactions:

1. Choose Lists > Scheduled Transactions. A window appears showing you your upcoming transactions (**Figure 7.8**). The window shows recurring transactions with their frequency, so rather than listing every future instance of a transaction that happens twice a month, it only lists the transaction's next due date and "Twice a month" in the Frequency column.

2. You can create a new scheduled transaction or edit or delete existing transactions using the buttons at the bottom of the Scheduled Transactions window.

Figure 7.7 Double-click on a day in the Calendar window to open the Transactions window that lists all transactions scheduled for or that occurred on that day.

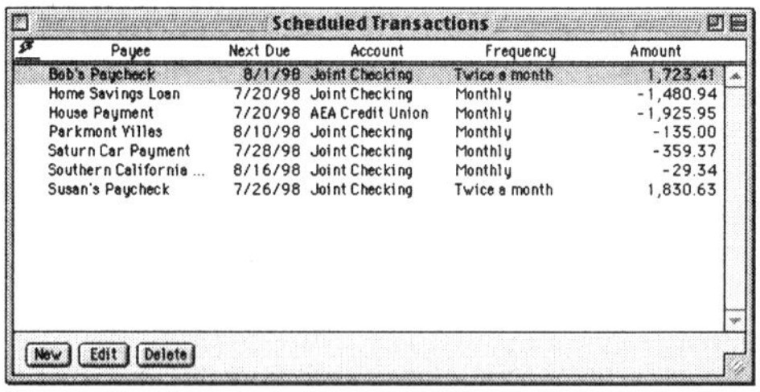

Figure 7.8 You can view upcoming transactions in the Scheduled Transactions window.

To delete a transaction:

1. In the Financial Calendar, double-click on the day that contains a transaction that you want to delete. The Transaction window for that day appears (see **Figure 7.7**).

2. Click the transaction to select it.

3. Click the Delete button in the Transactions window.

4. Quicken will ask you to confirm the deletion. Click the Yes button to delete the transaction.

5. Close the Transactions window.

✔ Tip

■ Remember that entering a transaction in the Calendar also enters it in an account register.

DELETE A TRANSACTION

Transaction Groups

It's often more convenient to pay your bills in batches. For example, I have three telephone lines at my house, so I receive three different bills. Because I prefer to pay all three bills at the same time, I've created a transaction group in the Calendar that automatically enters three separate transactions simultaneously.

To create a transaction group:

1. Choose Lists > Transaction Groups. The Transaction Groups window appears, as shown in **Figure 7.9**.

2. Click the New button. The Set Up Group window appears, as shown in **Figure 7.10**.

3. In the field next to Group Name, type in a name for the transaction group.

4. From the pop-up menu next to Destination, choose the account from which the payments will be made.

5. In the Reminder Settings section, set the frequency for which the group transaction should recur, and then enter the next date for the group transaction.

6. Select the transactions that you want to include in the group. A check mark appears next to each selected transaction. If you make a mistake and need to deselect a transaction, click it again to remove the check mark.

7. Click the Create button.

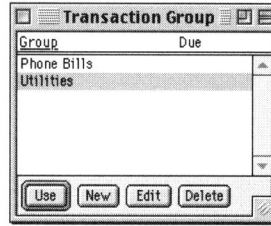

Figure 7.9 The Transactions Group window lets you view old groups or add new ones.

Figure 7.10 You can set up a transaction group in the Set Up Group window.

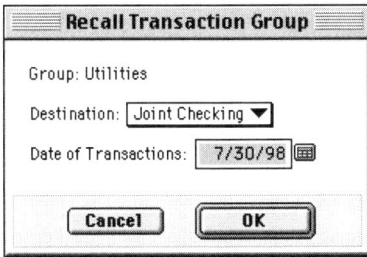

Figure 7.11 The Recall Transaction Group dialog lets you add multiple entries in the account register in one step.

To use a transaction group:

1. In the Transaction Group window, select a transaction group.

2. Click the Use button. The Recall Transaction Group dialog box appears (**Figure 7.11**).

3. Check that the settings in the dialog box are correct, and then click the OK button. Quicken will make the appropriate entries in the account register(s) and then open those registers for your inspection. If necessary, edit the transactions in the registers in the usual fashion.

Adding Calendar Notes

In addition to showing transactions, the Calendar can also contain notes, kind of like yellow sticky notes, that contain virtually any information—from personal notes to to-do lists to additional notes on the financial transactions for that day.

To create a calendar note:

1. In the Calendar window, select a date to which you wish to add a note.

2. At the bottom of the Calendar window, click the Add Note button. The note window for that date appears.

3. Enter the text for the note (**Figure 7.12**).

4. Close the window to save the note.

5. Quicken adds a small note icon to the day in which you created the note (**Figure 7.13**). To read the note in the future, double-click the note icon.

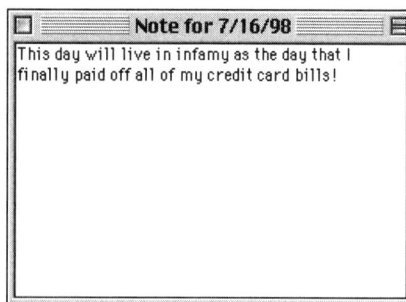

Figure 7.12 You can include any text that you want in the Calendar's note window.

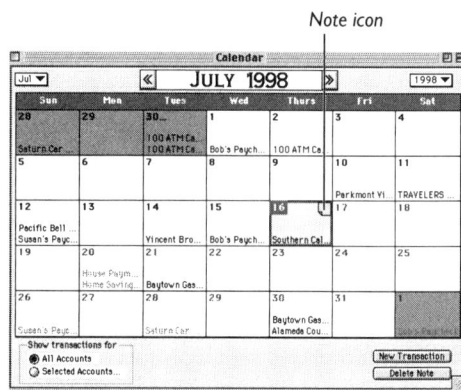

Figure 7.13 Double-click the note icon to recall your note.

BALANCING
YOUR ACCOUNTS

Balancing your checkbook is one of Those Chores—things that everyone knows you need to do, that everyone claims to do regularly, but that surprisingly few people actually do. And who can blame them? Balancing your checkbook by hand is a pain, especially if you have slacked off for a few months and need to catch up.

Tracking your checking account and balancing your checkbook is the number one reason why people buy Quicken. Quicken does a great job of reconciling accounts, and it makes a chore that took an hour by hand easy to do in just a few minutes.

Quicken isn't limited to just reconciling your checkbook, however. You can balance your savings, money market, or credit card accounts too. In addition to balancing accounts, you can update balances in cash, asset, or liability accounts to reflect transfers of funds, payments made, or interest received.

In this chapter, you'll learn how to reconcile accounts, update account balances, and resolve any differences between the bank's records and your own.

Balancing Accounts

You'll use the same procedure to balance a checking account, a savings account, or a money market account. First you enter your bank statement balance, and then you match transactions on your bank statement with transactions in your Quicken account register.

Balancing a credit card account works in almost the same way—except that if a balance is due on the credit card, Quicken will ask whether you want to make a payment at the end of the reconciliation process.

Before you begin, you should make sure that you have entered all transactions that occurred between the date of your last statement and the date of your current statement.

If you need to reconcile for more than one month, you first need to reconcile your account with the bank statements for each of the prior months before you try to reconcile the current month's statement.

To balance a checking, savings, or money market account:

1. Click the Banking button (**Figure 8.1**) in the activity bar to open the banking area.

2. From the Registers pop-up menu in the task bar, select the account that you wish to reconcile (**Figure 8.2**). The account register appears.

3. Click the Reconcile button in the task bar (**Figure 8.3**). The Reconcile Startup window appears (**Figure 8.4**).

4. Check to make sure that the beginning balance on your bank statement matches the amount in the Beginning Balance box in the Reconcile Startup window. If the amounts don't match, you'll need to click the Cancel button and fix the problem.

Figure 8.1 Click the Banking button in the activity bar to open the banking area.

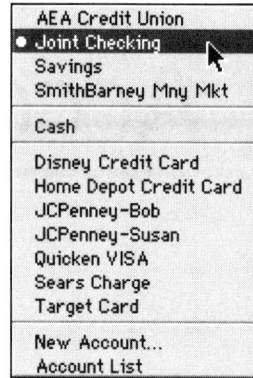

Figure 8.2 Select the account that you wish to reconcile.

Figure 8.3 Click the Reconcile button to open the Reconcile Startup window.

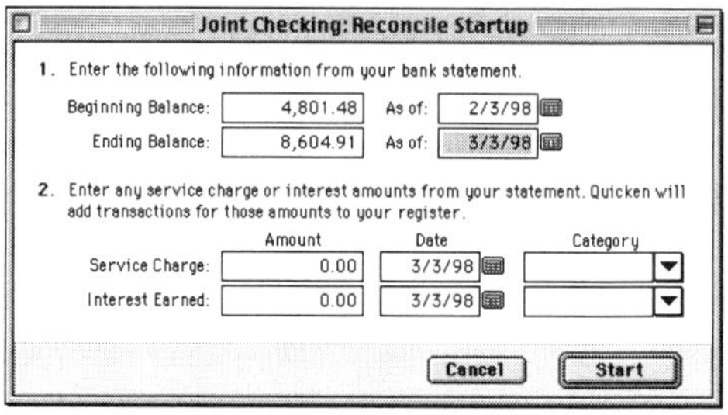

Figure 8.4 Check to make sure that the beginning balance on your bank statement matches the amount in the Beginning Balance box.

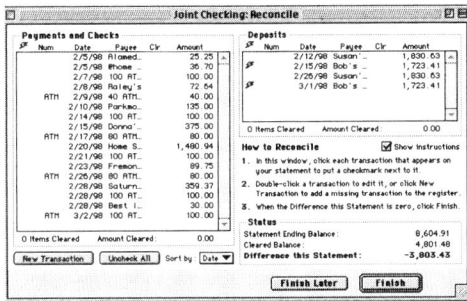

Figure 8.5 Click each transaction that has cleared on your bank statement in the Reconcile window.

Figure 8.6 Click the OK button in the Reconcile Complete window.

5. Enter the Ending Balance from your bank statement.

6. Enter the amount, date, and category of service charges or interest transactions.

7. Click the Start button. The Reconcile window appears (**Figure 8.5**).

8. Click each transaction that has cleared on your bank statement. A checkmark appears next to each cleared transaction.

9. Double-click on any transaction in error in the Reconcile window to open the account register and edit it. To add a missing transaction, click the New Transaction button at the bottom of the window to open the account register and make the addition.

10. As you check off each transaction, Quicken updates the "Difference this Statement" figure in the right lower corner of the window. When you've checked off all the transactions, that figure should be zero. If it is, click the Finish button.

    If a difference amount still appears, skip to "Correcting Differences" later in this chapter to find out how to correct the problem.

11. If you balance successfully, the Reconcile Complete window appears (**Figure 8.6**). Click the OK button.

✔ Tips

■ At the bottom of the Reconcile window (**Figure 8.5**), the "Sort by" pop-up menu lets you sort items in the lists by number or by date.

■ Reconciliation problems occur for a variety of reasons, but it's usually that a previous month was not reconciled. See the Quicken User Manual for details on fixing beginning balance problems.

BALANCING ACCOUNTS

To balance a credit card account:

1. Credit card accounts are balanced in almost the same way as checking, savings, or money market accounts. Follow steps 1 through 10 above using a credit card account.

2. If you balance successfully, the Reconcile Complete window appears, which looks a bit different for credit card accounts (**Figure 8.7**).

3. If you want a make a payment on your credit card at this time, click the Yes button. The Pay Credit/Charge Card window appears (**Figure 8.8**).

4. Select the account you wish to pay from, then select the means of payment using the "Handwritten," "Printed," or "Electronic" radio button.

5. Choose the amount you will pay by selecting the "Minimum," "Full," or "Other" radio button. If you select "Other," fill in the amount you wish to pay in the box.

6. Click the Pay button. Quicken enters the payment in the register for the account you selected.

Figure 8.7 Just as with your checking account, after you balance your credit card account successfully, the Reconcile Complete window appears.

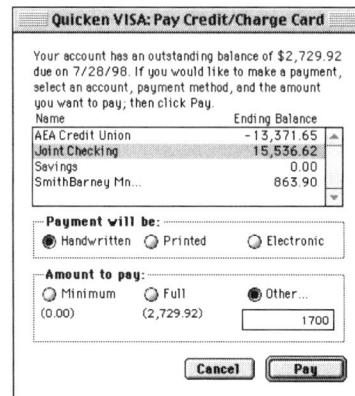

Figure 8.8 Click the Yes button to make a payment to your credit card account.

Correcting Differences

In the Reconcile window, if the "Difference this Statement" amount is not zero, it means that your account is not balancing for the current statement period. This usually occurs for one of two reasons: either a wrong number of payment or deposit items have been checked or some of the checked items have incorrect dollar amounts.

To find the mistakes:

1. Count the number of credit items on your bank statement, and then count the number of deposits shown in the Reconcile window. If the number doesn't match, you've found the problem.

   Or

   Compare the number of checks and payments on your bank statement against the number of debit items in the Reconcile window. You might not have recorded an item in the register, or you might have duplicated a transaction, entered a payment as a deposit or a deposit as a payment, or marked an item cleared by mistake.

2. If the number of items is correct but the statement still doesn't balance, you have a problem with the dollar amount of one or more of your items. By hand or using a calculator, add up all the transactions shown under "Payments and Checks."

3. Compare the total with the total of debits on the statement. If the numbers don't match, you have a problem with the dollar amount of the debits.

4. Add up all the transactions shown under "Deposits" and compare them to the total of deposits on the statement. If those numbers don't match, there's a discrepancy in your deposit figures.

Letting Quicken fix the problem

If the dollar amount of an unreconciled balance is small, you may decide that it's not worth the time it takes to track down the mistake. In that case, you can let Quicken enter a register adjustment, which will force your account to reconcile.

If you click the Finish button in the Reconcile window while there is still a difference, Quicken will pop up the Adjust Ending Balance window (**Figure 8.9**). If you want Quicken to enter an account adjustment, click the "Adjust Register" button. If you want to take another whack at finding the mistake, click the "Return to Reconcile" button.

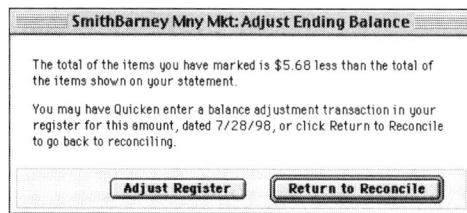

✔ Tips

■ The most common mistake in this area seems to be transposing two digits during data entry.

■ If you're off a fairly small amount that is an even number (for example, $8.00, rather than $3.87), it's likely that you missed entering a bank service charge of some sort. Check your statement carefully for charges you don't normally see, such as for check printing or using another bank's ATM.

■ Using Online Banking (see Chapter 9) makes balancing your checkbook and other accounts even easier, because you download your bank and credit card statements directly into Quicken's account registers.

Figure 8.9 To have Quicken enter a balance adjustment for an account that just won't balance, click the Adjust Register button.

BANKING AND PAYING BILLS ONLINE

Using your computer to download bank statements and pay bills is a new and, to some people, a scary way of dealing with your bank. Yet it can save you a lot of time and a bit of money.

Doing your banking online can save you time because you don't need to hand record your checks, ATM withdrawals, or credit card transactions. Instead, you download them from your bank, review the transactions to catch any possible errors and make sure they are properly categorized, and then add them to your account registers with the click of a button. Because the information is current as of the close of the previous banking day, you can monitor your cash flow more closely. This lets you make sure, for example, that deposits are credited to your account before you write checks and helps you to avoid expensive bounced check charges.

Online bill payment lets you transfer money from your checking account directly to your creditors. You don't have to write or print checks, stuff envelopes, find stamps, or go to the post office. You simply enter a payment in an account register and have Quicken send it over the phone lines.

Setting up Online Banking

To use online banking, you must first have access to the Internet. You'll need an Internet Service Provider (ISP) and a modem or another connection to the Internet. You can also access the Internet if you have an America Online or a CompuServe account. You need to tell Quicken what sort of Internet connection you have. Additionally, if you tell Quicken which Web browser you're using, Quicken can use the browser to show you information on Intuit's Web site about how apply for online banking.

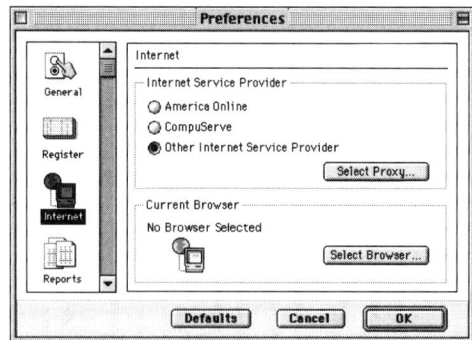
Figure 9.1 Select the Internet icon from the scrolling list on the left of the Preferences window.

To set Quicken's Internet preferences:

1. Choose Edit > Preferences to open the Preferences window (**Figure 9.1**). Then select the Internet icon from the scrolling list on the left.

2. Select the ISP you're using.

3. Click the Select Browser button. The open file dialog box appears (**Figure 9.2**).

4. Select the appropriate browser, and then click the Open button.

5. Click the OK button to save your Internet preferences.

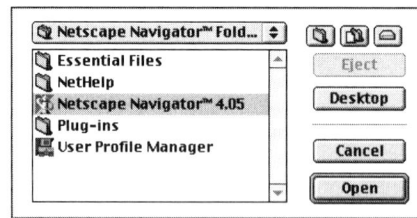
Figure 9.2 Select the appropriate browser in the open file dialog box.

Why not use the Web?

Some banks now allow you to view accounts and make transactions over the World Wide Web, rather than download transactions into Quicken. Web access is nice for quick checks of account balances, but it's inferior to downloading into Quicken. Why? The main reason is speed. The Web way is slo-o-o-o-w. And if you view information on the Web using your Web browser, you still have the problem of entering that data into your registers. On the other hand, downloading a month's worth of transactions into Quicken takes less than a minute. The direct download method works much better.

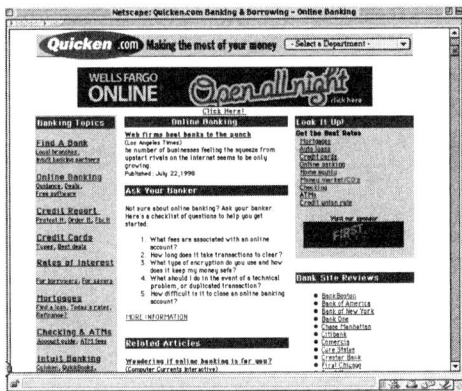

Figure 9.3 Quicken.com provides a wealth of useful information when you're shopping for an institution that offers online banking—or even just considering the option.

Applying for Online Banking

You must contact your bank or other financial institution to get online access for checking, savings, and credit card accounts. Not all financial institutions support online banking, and some support online banking only for certain account types, such as checking but not credit card accounts. Even if your financial institution doesn't support online banking, you can still use online bill payment through Intuit. If you have accounts at more than one financial institution, you'll need to apply to each one separately.

Each financial institution sets its own fees for online banking. The fee amount varies from bank to bank, so it's a good idea to shop around for the best deal. You can find a list of banks and their online banking fees on Intuit's Web site at **http://www.quicken.com.** Look for the Banking & Borrowing section, and then look for Online Banking (see **Figure 9.3**).

After you have signed up for online banking, your financial institution sends you a kit with the information that you'll need to set up your Quicken accounts for online banking. You'll also receive an initial personal identification number (PIN), which you should change in your first online banking session.

To enable a Quicken account for online use:

1. Choose Online > Enable Online Banking > Online Banking. The Select Account to Enable window appears (**Figure 9.4**).

2. Select the account you want to set up for online service, and then click OK. The Enable Online Banking window appears (**Figure 9.5**).

3. Click the "Enable account access" check box if you'll be using this account to download statements. Click the "Enable online payment" check box to use the account for bill payments.

4. Refer to the information kit you received from your financial institution to enter the financial institution name, routing number, account number, and account type, exactly as listed in the kit.

5. Enter your Social Security number.

6. Click the Save button. You return to the Select Account to Enable window, which now shows a lighting bolt next to the account name indicating that it is enabled for online services.

7. Repeat steps 2 through 6 to enable other accounts.

Online-enabled accounts

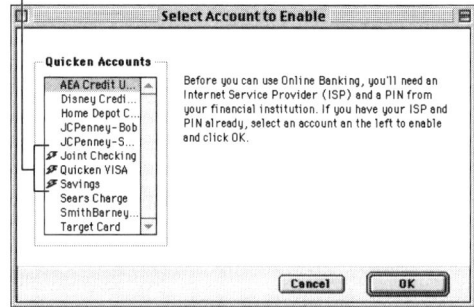

Figure 9.4 Select the account you want to set up for online service.

Figure 9.5 Click a check box to indicate what action you want Quicken to take.

Figure 9.6 Switch to the banking area by clicking the Banking button in the activity bar.

Figure 9.7 Click the Download button to open the Download Transactions window.

Financial institution pop-up menu

Accept items button

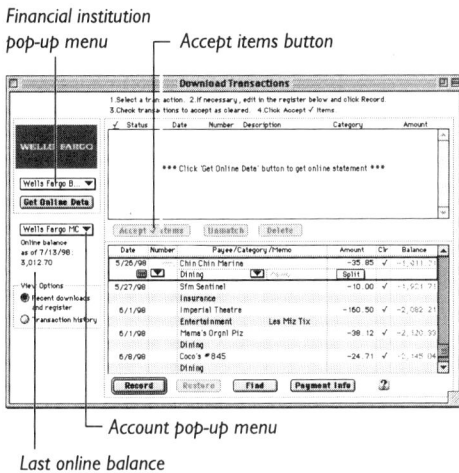

Account pop-up menu

Last online balance

Figure 9.8 Start your online transaction from the Download Transactions window.

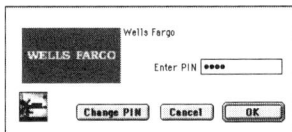

Figure 9.9 Enter your PIN and click the OK button.

Going Online

The first time that you go online, it's a good idea to just download your current transactions. This gets you used to the process and lets you update your account registers. During this first session, your bank may prompt you to change your PIN.

To download transactions:

1. Switch to the banking area by clicking the Banking button in the activity bar (**Figure 9.6**).

2. Click the Download button in the task bar (**Figure 9.7**), or choose Online > Download Transactions. The Download Transactions window appears (**Figure 9.8**).

3. If you have online accounts at more than one financial institution, choose the financial institution you want from the pop-up menu below the institution's logo on the left side of the window.

   Click the Get Online Data button. Quicken connects to the Internet and then asks for your PIN (**Figure 9.9**).

4. Enter your PIN, and then click the OK button.

5. The Online Transmission Summary window will appear (**Figure 9.10**). Review the information, and then click the OK button.

Quicken displays the downloaded transactions in the top half of the Download Transactions window. You can sort the downloaded transactions by clicking one of the column titles.

6. Quicken compares the downloaded transactions with transactions that are already in your account register. If the transactions correspond, the word "Match" appears next to the downloaded transaction in the Download Transaction window. Click each matched transaction to place a checkmark next to it, signifying that it is ready to be cleared in your register.

7. If Quicken doesn't find a match for a downloaded transaction, the transaction appears in the list in the Status column marked "New." Quicken marks a transaction as New when you haven't yet entered that transaction in your account register or when the check number or amount differs from the transaction that you entered. For these New transactions, you'll need to enter the missing payee and/or category information. Select the New transaction in the transaction list. Quicken displays the transaction in the register at the bottom of the Download Transactions window.

8. Make your changes in the register, and then click the Record button. The transaction's status will change to "Match." Click the newly matched transaction to place a checkmark next to it.

Figure 9.10 Review the information in the Online Transmission Summary window and then click OK.

Is Online Banking Secure?

Since online banking and online bill payment transactions travel over the Internet, it's perfectly reasonable to wonder if your financial data can be intercepted and used by criminals. Quicken's security measures make it extremely unlikely.

The first line of defense is the Personal Identification Number (PIN) that you must enter whenever you use online banking or bill payment. When you first sign up for online banking, your bank sends you a PIN that you can (and should) change. After you change it, you're the only one who knows that PIN. For extra security, you should change your PIN on a regular basis.

For additional security, Quicken encrypts all transferred information—back and forth. *Encryption* is a technique that scrambles data before it is sent using a mathematical algorithm. At the other end, your bank unscrambles the data. (For those more technically inclined, Quicken uses 128-bit DES (Data Encryption Standard) encryption along with SSL (Secure Sockets Layer) transfer protocols.)

9. Repeat steps 8 and 9 for every New transaction.

10. Click the Accept Items button.

Quicken adds the checked items to the account register marked cleared and removes them from the transaction list in the Download Transactions window.

✔ Tips

- Your financial institution may label ATM transactions and service charges as EFT, which stands for Electronic Funds Transfer.

- Quicken doesn't close the Internet connection after it finishes downloading, so if you're using a dial-up connection, you must close it manually.

- You can edit your transactions to change the category either before or after updating your register, but it's usually easier to do it in the Download Transactions window.

GOING ONLINE

Paying Bills Online

To make online bill payments with Quicken, you'll first need to set up the payment recipients in the Payee list. To send a payment, you just select a payee from the list, create the payment instruction, and send it to your financial institution.

To set up a payee:

1. Choose Online > Payments > Online Payees. The Payees window appears (**Figure 9.11**).

2. Click the New button. The Set Up Payee window appears (**Figure 9.12**).

3. Enter the payee's name, address, and phone number.

4. Enter the account number that the payee uses to identify you. If the payee doesn't use account numbers, enter your name.

5. Click the Create button. Quicken will present a dialog box asking you to review and verify the payee information. If it is correct, click the Yes button; otherwise, click the No button and correct the payee information. After you verify the information, Quicken adds the new payee to the Payee list.

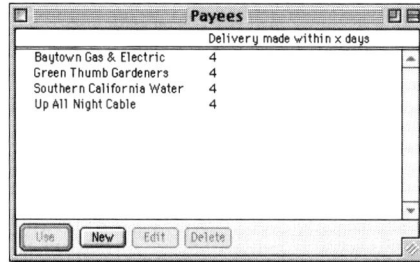

Figure 9.11 Click the New button to open the Set Up Payee window.

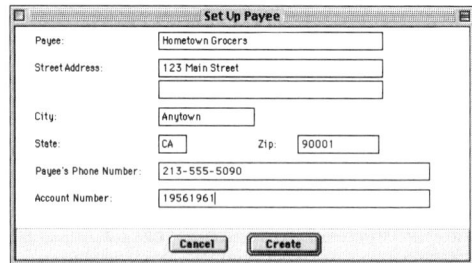

Figure 9.12 Enter the payee's information and account number.

Figure 9.13 Click the Payment button in the task bar to open the Enter Online Payment window.

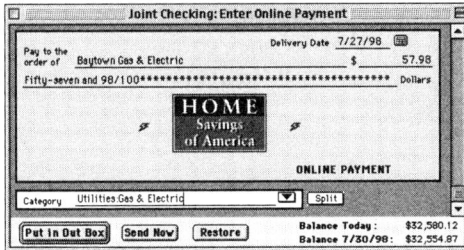

Figure 9.14 Select a payee and click Use.

Figure 9.15 Click the Out Box button in the task bar to open the Out Box.

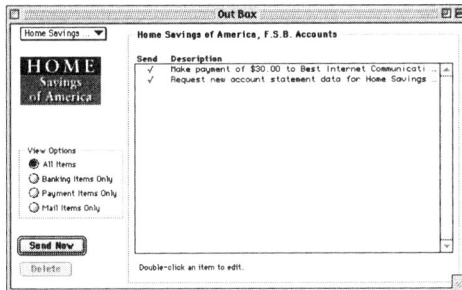

Figure 9.16 Review the items in the Out Box and click Send Now.

To create and send an online payment:

1. Click the Banking button in the activity bar to switch to the banking section.

2. Click the Registers button in the task bar, and choose the account from which you want to make the online payment.

3. Choose Online > Payments > Online Payees. The Payees window appears.

4. Click the Payment button in the task bar (**Figure 9.13**). The Enter Online Payment window appears (**Figure 9.14**).

5. In the Payees window, select one of the payees, and then click the Use button. The payee's name is transferred to the Enter Online Payment window.

6. Fill in the amount and the category in the Enter Online Payment window.

7. If you plan to create more online payments in the current session, click the Put in Out Box button. Quicken stores the payment in a list of instructions to send to your financial institution the next time you connect. If this is the only payment you are making, click the Send Now button. Quicken immediately connects online, prompts you for your PIN, and sends your payment instruction.

8. If you put payments into the Out Box, click the Out Box button in the task bar (**Figure 9.15**). The Out Box appears (**Figure 9.16**).

9. Review the items in the Out Box, and if you're satisfied, click the Send Now button. Quicken connects to your financial institution and sends the payments.

✔ Tips

- If your payee is set up to receive electronic funds transfers, payment is transferred directly from your account to your payee's account. This usually takes less than two business days. If the payee doesn't accept EFTs, your financial institution prints a check and sends it to the payee by U.S. mail. It's important that you allow sufficient time for the payment to get to the payee to avoid a late charge. So make sure that you schedule payments at least three or four days before a payment due date.

- Don't forget that a payee will often need a day or two after receiving a check to process the payment and credit your account.

10

CREATING REPORTS

I have to admit that before I started using Quicken, my financial house was not exactly in order. Like many people, I had built up a bit too much credit card debt; I balanced my checkbook twice a year, whether it needed it or not; and although I knew that money was coming in and money was going out, I didn't know just where all that money was going.

Quicken's reports, one of its most powerful tools, went a long way toward solving my financial problems by giving me a comprehensive picture of my finances. After using Quicken for just a few months, I had a good record of how much I was spending and where I was spending it. I could also see how much I was spending on interest, which really gave me the impetus to pay off those bills.

One of the best features of Quicken reports is that you can use them to look at your financial data in different ways. You can view your finances in as much or as little detail as you need, and you can pull out just the information that you want. For example, at tax time, I pull a report to show all of my tax-deductible expenditures for the previous year, all neatly categorized and totaled. My accountant appreciates it (anything would be better than that shoe box of loose receipts I use to drop on his desk), and because using the reports takes less of his time, it saves me money.

Using Reports

Quicken comes with a variety of report templates that cover most of the questions you have about your finances. You can customize those reports to zero in on just the information that you want.

You can get six kinds of reports from Quicken: EasyAnswer reports, QuickReports, Standard reports, Memorized reports, Shortcut reports, and Register and List reports.

You use a slightly different method to create each kind of report. You can move among different kinds of reports by using the tabs at the top of the Reports window. The scrolling window at the left side of the window displays the names of Quicken's report templates. When you click on the name of a report template, Quicken shows you a sample of that report on the right side of the Reports window.

Figure 10.1 Click the Reporting button in the activity bar to switch among Quicken's Reports area.

Figure 10.2 Click the Reports button in the task bar to open the Reports window.

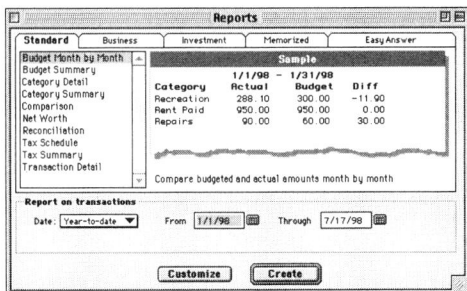

Figure 10.3 The Reports window gives you access to a wide variety of report templates.

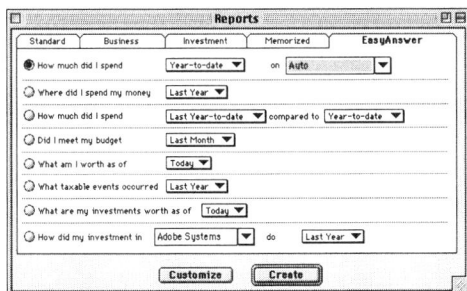

Figure 10.4 EasyAnswer reports offer quick and basic information about your finances.

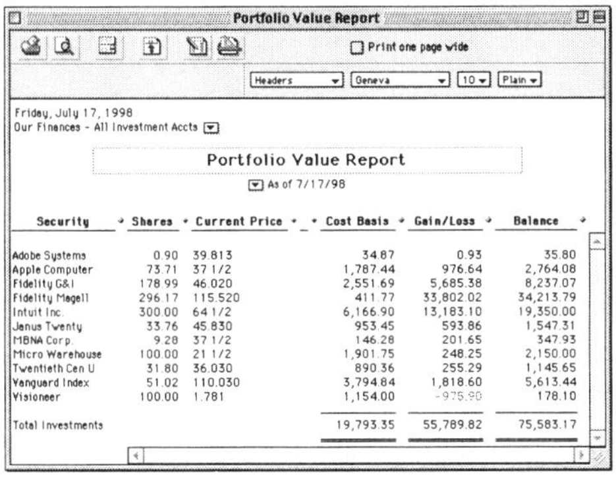

Figure 10.5 An example of a Quicken report.

Using EasyAnswer Reports

EasyAnswer reports give you quick answers to eight basic questions, such as "Where did I spend my money?" and "What are my investments worth?"

To create an EasyAnswer report:

1. Click the Reporting button in the activity bar (**Figure 10.1**).

2. Click the Reports button in the task bar (**Figure 10.2**). The Reports window appears (**Figure 10.3**).

3. Click on the EasyAnswer tab. Quicken displays the EasyAnswer report window (**Figure 10.4**). This window shows eight basic questions that you can ask about your finances. Select the radio button with the question that you want to ask.

4. If necessary, adjust the date range by choosing a new time frame from the pop-up menu next to the radio button that you clicked.

5. If you picked a question that requires it, choose a category to narrow your report from the pop-up menu next to the question.

6. Click the Create button. Quicken displays the report on your screen (**Figure 10.5**).

Using QuickReport

A QuickReport is a transaction detail report that offers only a few options; it's designed to give you fast information for one specific payee, category, account, or security.

To create a QuickReport:

1. Click the QuickReport button in the task bar (**Figure 10.6**). The Create QuickReport dialog box appears (**Figure 10.7**).

2. Choose the source for the report using the pop-up menu. Your choices are Payee & Description, Category, Class, Memo, Account, or Security.

3. Type in your search criteria.

4. Choose the date range for the QuickReport from the pop-up menu next to Date.

5. Click the OK button. Quicken grinds through its data file and presents a transaction report based on your criteria (**Figure 10.8**).

Figure 10.6 Click the QuickReport button in the task bar to open the QuickReport dialog box.

Figure 10.7 Enter information in the Create QuickReport dialog box for fast report results.

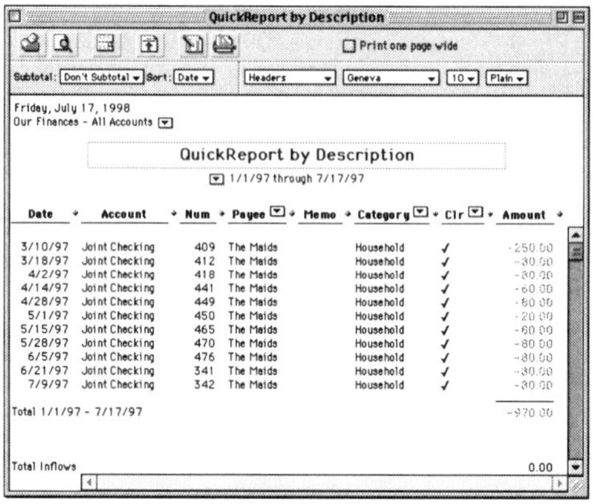

Figure 10.8 A transaction report created with the QuickReport feature. In this report, we searched for all transactions from last year-to-date where the category was Household.

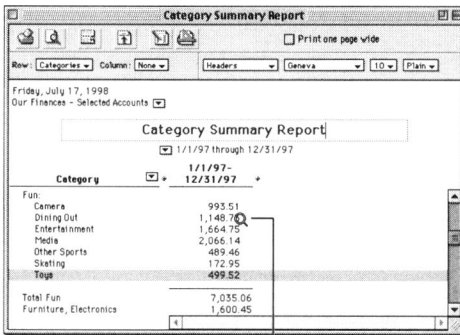

Magnifying-glass cursor

Figure 10.9 When the cursor turns into a magnifying glass, you can zoom in for more detailed information by double-clicking.

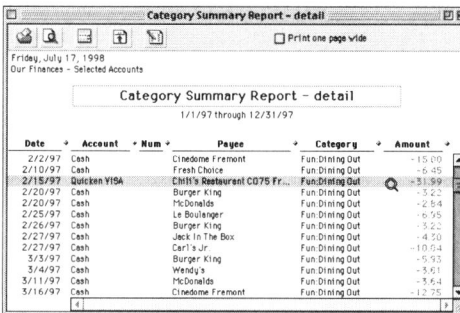

Figure 10.10 The detail transaction report produced by zooming in on a category—in this case, Fun.

Figure 10.11 Zooming further, the final level of detail shows the original transaction in the account register.

Zooming in on the Details

You can use QuickZoom to examine the information in your reports in greater detail. If you're viewing a report that summarizes the amounts from a category, you can double-click on an amount and QuickZoom will take you to another report that shows more detail about the item you selected. But if you use QuickZoom in a transaction report, Quicken opens the register and shows you the original transaction.

To use QuickZoom:

1. Create a report summarizing expenses by category. (You can actually create any sort of report you wish.)

2. In the open report window, move the cursor over one of the amounts in the report until the cursor turns into a magnifying glass (**Figure 10.9**).

3. Double-click on the amount of a category. A new transaction report window opens showing you the detailed transactions for the category (**Figure 10.10**).

4. To view an original transaction, double-click on an amount in the detailed transaction report window. The account register for the transaction will open, with the transaction selected (**Figure 10.11**).

USING QUICKREPORT

81

Using Standard Reports

Standard reports give you basic information, such as details of transactions, net worth, and category transaction reports. In the tabs at the top of the Reports window, Quicken lists Standard, Business, and Investment report types. All three of these types are generated in the same fashion.

To create a Standard report:

1. Click the Reporting button in the activity bar.

2. Click the Reports button in the task bar. The Reports window appears (**Figure 10.12**).

3. Click on the Standard, Business, or Investment tabs at the top of the Reports window. The window will switch to the area you clicked.

4. In the scrolling pane on the left side of the window, select a template for a report that you want to create. On the right side of the window, Quicken shows you a sample of the kind of report you select.

5. If necessary, change the date range of the report by changing the value of the Date pop-up menu or by typing in a date or dates in the date field in the Reports window.

6. Click the Create button to generate the report (**Figure 10.13**).

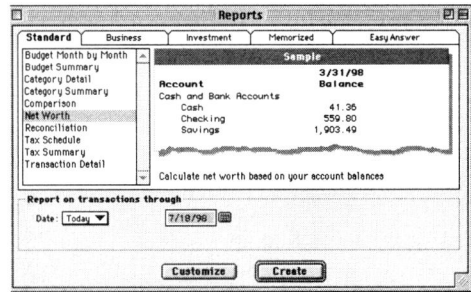

Figure 10.12 You can change the date range of a report by typing in a new date or by choosing a new value in the Date pop-up menu.

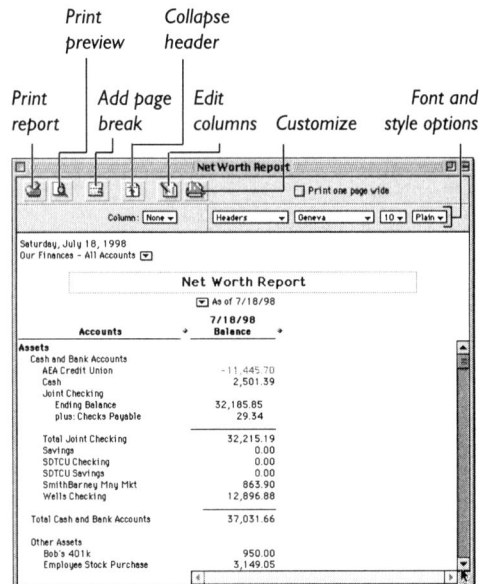

Figure 10.13 A typical report window.

Figure 10.14 Select an option from the Row pop-up menu to change the contents of the rows in a report.

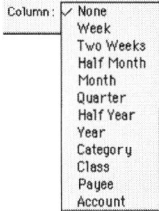

Figure 10.15 Select an option from the Column pop-up menu to choose the contents of the columns in the report.

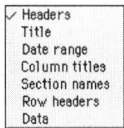

Figure 10.16 These pop-up menus let you change the look of the text in each part of a report.

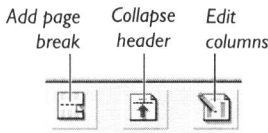

Add page break   Collapse header   Edit columns

Figure 10.17 Use these icons to customize the overall look of the report.

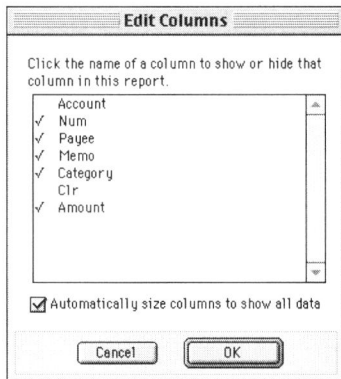

Figure 10.18 The Edit Columns window lets you choose which columns to include in your report.

Customizing Reports

You can customize reports in Quicken in two ways: by creating a custom layout of a Standard report or by creating an entirely new custom report.

To customize report layouts:

1. Follow steps 1 through 6 in the section above, "Creating Standard reports."

2. In the Report window, choose one or more of the following formatting options:

   - Change the contents of the rows in a report by selecting an option from the Row pop-up menu **(Figure 10.14).**

   - Choose the contents of the columns in the report by selecting an option from the Column pop-up menu **(Figure 10.15)**.

   - Change the look of the text in the report by selecting options from the font, font size, and style pop-up menus **(Figure 10.16)**.

   - Click the "Print one page wide" check box to ask Quicken to resize the report to fit on one page.

   - Edit the report title by selecting it and typing in a new one.

   - Resize the width of the columns in the report by clicking and dragging the diamonds between each column head. Drag the rules under each column head to rearrange the columns in the report.

✔ Tip

- You can also customize the look of the report by clicking on one of the three icons in the Report window **(Figure 10.17)**. To add a page break, select a row in the report and click on the Page Break icon. Click on the Collapse Header icon to remove the header from the printed document. Click on the Edit Columns icon to open a window that allows you to select which columns to include in your report **(Figure 10.18)**.

CUSTOMIZING REPORTS

To create a custom report:

1. Follow steps 1 through 4 in "Creating a Standard report" above to choose a report template.

2. Click the Customize button at the bottom of the Reports window. The Customize Report window appears.

3. Make changes in one or more of the following areas:

- The Layout tab (**Figure 10.19**) of the Customize Report window lets you specify row and column headings as well as the date range for the report.

- The Content tablets you choose which information will appear in the report. (**Figure 10.20**). You can narrow the focus of your report to show only the items of your interest.

- The Organization tab (**Figure 10.21**) allows you to organize the look of a report either as an income and expense report or by cash flow.

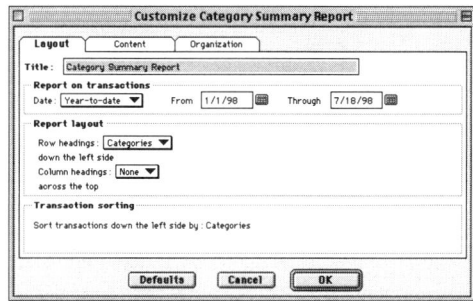

Figure 10.19 The Layout tab lets you set the basic report parameters.

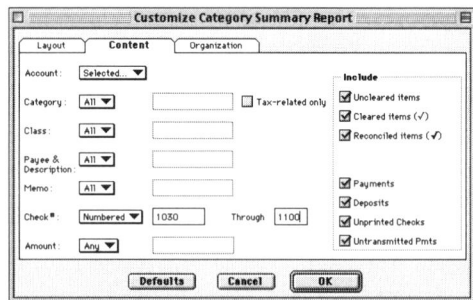

Figure 10.20 Narrow the report's information from the Content tab.

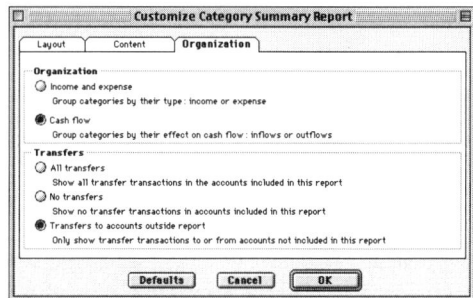

Figure 10.21 The Organization tab lets you switch between two different ways to view you report.

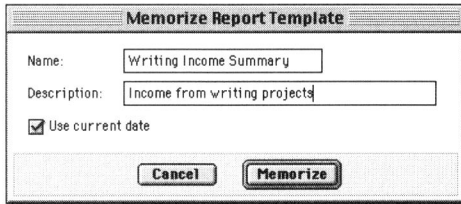

Figure 10.22 Enter the name of a memorized report in the Memorize Report Template window.

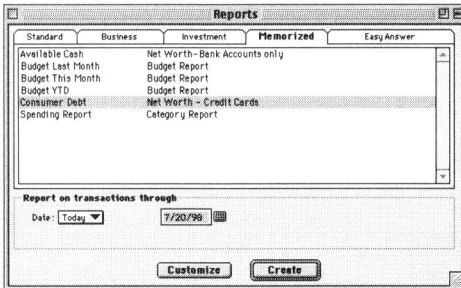

Figure 10.23 Choose a report that you have already memorized from the Memorized tab in the Reports window.

Using Memorized Reports

Tweaking reports until they're just the way that you want them can take some effort, and it would be a waste of your time if you had to re-create a custom report every time. Instead, you can save custom settings and reuse them. These are called Memorized reports.

To memorize a report:

1. Create a custom report.

2. Choose Edit > Memorize, or press Cmd-M. The Memorize Report Template window appears (**Figure 10.22**).

3. Enter a name and a description for the report. If you click the "Use current date" check box, Quicken will memorize the dates that you specified when you customized the report.

4. Click the Memorize button.

To use a memorized report:

1. Click the Reports button in the task bar.

2. In the Reports window, click on the Memorized tab (**Figure 10.23**).

3. Click on the memorized report that you want to use. Optionally, change the date range at the bottom of the Reports window.

4. Click the Create button.

✔ Tip

■ Quicken 98 has a bug that affects memorized dates. If you memorize a report calling for year-to-date results, Quicken remembers the date that you memorized the report but will not yield the correct year-to-date when you next use the report. So if you memorize a report on March 1 and run that report again on May 1, you'll still get March results. The solution is to change the dates manually when you re-run the memorized report.

Shortcut Reports

Shortcut reports are found in the account registers. They are simple year-to-date transaction reports of all occurrences of a selected payee or category.

To create a shortcut report:

1. Open an account register.

2. Scroll through the register until you find the transaction on which you want a report. Click on the transaction to select it.

3. When you selected the transaction, the Shortcuts pop-up menu appeared in that transaction (**Figure 10.24**). Click on the Shortcuts menu, and choose either "Report on [payee name]" or "Report on [category name]." Quicken generates the report (**Figure 10.25**).

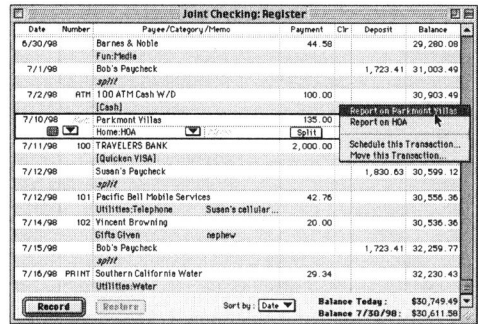

Figure 10.24 The Shortcuts pop-up menu in the account register lets you get fast reports on a transaction.

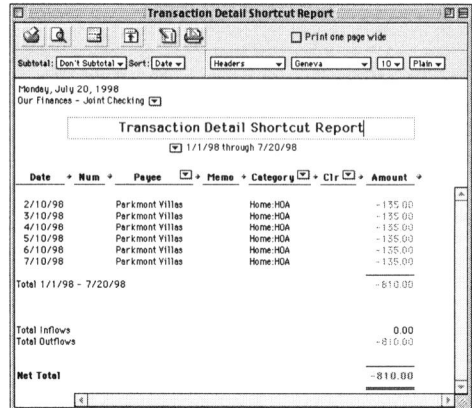

Figure 10.25 The Shortcuts Transaction Detail report gives you quick year-to-date information about the payee or category of a transaction.

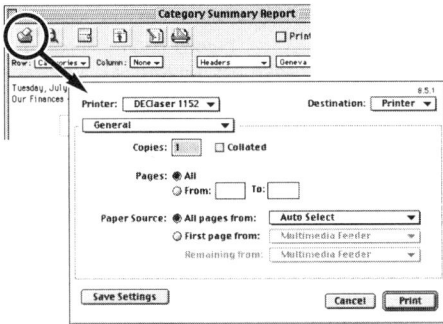

Figure 10.26 To print any type of Quicken report, choose File > Report or click the Print button at the top of the Reports window, and click Print.

Printing Reports

Quicken makes it easy to print reports and lists of all kinds, whether from the Reports section or from other areas of the program, such as account registers or lists.

To print a report:

1. Click the Reporting button in the activity bar.

2. Click the Reports button in the task bar to open the Reports window.

3. Create a standard or memorized report as described earlier in this chapter, or choose an existing report.

4. Choose File > Print Report. The printer dialog box will appear.

Or

Click the Print button at the top of the Reports window. The printer dialog box will appear, as shown in **Figure 10.26**.

5. Click the Print button to print your report.

✔ Tip

■ Note that Quicken, unlike almost every other Macintosh program, doesn't use Command-P as the shortcut key for its printing needs. That shortcut key is reserved for Print Checks.

Register and List Reports

These aren't exactly reports in the same sense as the the other five types. With these reports, Quicken simply allows you to print the current list or account register. But sometimes that's all you need.

To print an account register or a list:

1. Open the account register or list that you want to print.

2. If you're printing a register, choose File > Print Register (**Figure 10.27**). The Print Register window will appear (**Figure 10.28**). Enter the date range of the register entries you wish to print, then click the OK button. If you are printing a list, the menu item will be called File > Print [*List Name*] ([*List Name*] is the name of the list you have open.)

3. The printer dialog box will appear.

4. Click the Print button.

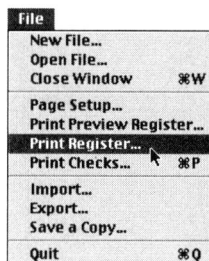

Figure 10.27 Sometimes it's handy to have a hard copy of all or part of a transactions register. That's easily accomplished, simply by choosing Print Register from the File menu.

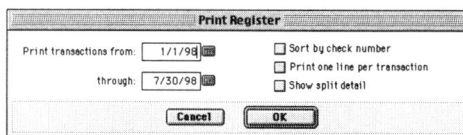

Figure 10.28 You can print out an entire history of your transactions from a given register, or specify a range of dates, using the two pop-up calendars or entering the dates in the windows.

CREATING GRAPHS

When it comes to getting a good overview of your finances, reports are good but graphs are better. Graphs can often illustrate relationships in your finances that numeric reports don't make clear.

Quicken can display your financial data as bar graphs, line graphs, and pie charts to help you quickly analyze your income and expenses, develop budgets, and determine your net worth.

In addition to their informational benefits, graphs can give you an important emotional boost, as I discovered while working to pay off my consumer debt. I created a bar graph that showed how much debt I owed. Every month, as I made payments, I'd check the graph to see how much the debt bar had shrunk. It felt great to see the downward trend in graphic form as I worked toward my goals—and it felt even better the month that the bar finally hit the zero mark.

As with reports (see Chapter 10 for more about reports), Quicken comes with a variety of templates to get you started using graphs. You can create custom graphs to answer particular questions about your finances. Quicken has three main types of graphs: *EasyAnswer* graphs, *Standard* graphs, and *Memorized* graphs.

Using EasyAnswer Graphs

EasyAnswer graphs address basic questions about your finances.

To create an EasyAnswer graph:

1. Click the Reporting button in the activity bar (**Figure 11.1**).

2. Click the Graphs button in the task bar (**Figure 11.2**). The Graphs window appears (**Figure 11.3**).

3. Click on the EasyAnswer tab. Quicken shows you the EasyAnswer Graphs window (**Figure 11.4**).

4. Select the radio button to indicate the question that you want to ask.

5. If necessary, choose a new time frame from the pop-up menu next to the radio button that you clicked.

6. If your question requires a category selection, choose one from the pop-up menu next to the selected question.

7. Click the Create button. Quicken displays the graph on your screen (**Figure 11.5**).

To use QuickZoom to get details:

1. Move the cursor over one of the colored areas on an existing graph. The cursor will turn into a magnifying glass. Click and hold the mouse button to see the dollar value of that segment of the graph (**Figure 11.6**).

2. Double-click on a segment of the graph to open another graph showing you more detail (**Figure 11.7**).

3. For even more detail, double-click on a segment of the detailed graph. A report window opens, showing you the original transactions that make up the graph segment (**Figure 11.8**).

Figure 11.1 Click this button to switch to Quicken's reporting area.

Figure 11.2 Click this button to open the Graphs window.

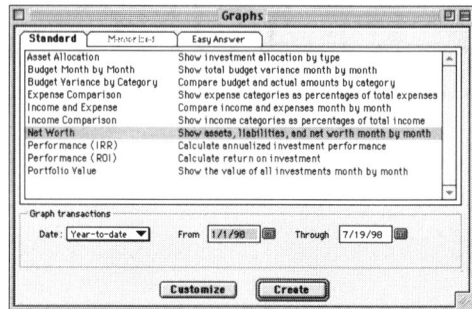

Figure 11.3 You create all of your graphs in Quicken from the Graphs window.

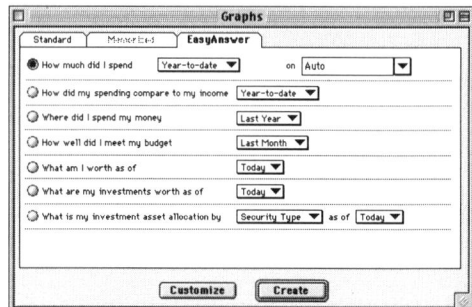

Figure 11.4 Use the EasyAnswer Graphs screen to get fast financial graphs.

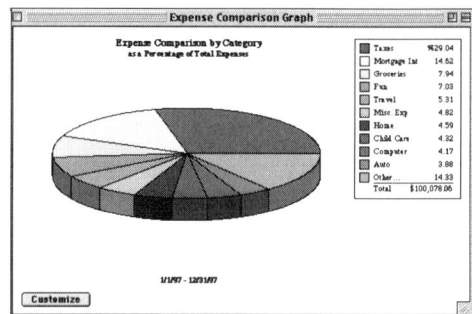

Figure 11.5 Quicken displays a completed graph.

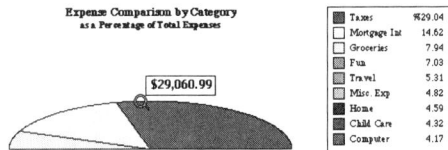

Figure 11.6 Click and hold down the mouse button when the cursor becomes a magnifying glass to see the dollar value of the graph segment.

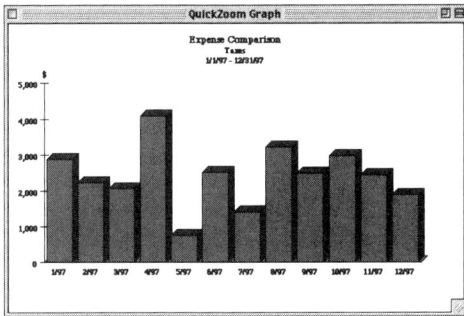

Figure 11.7 Double-click on the graph segment to open a more detailed graph.

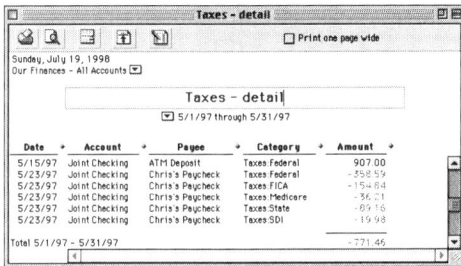

Figure 11.8 Double-click on the detailed to see a report showing you the original transactions that were used to create the graph.

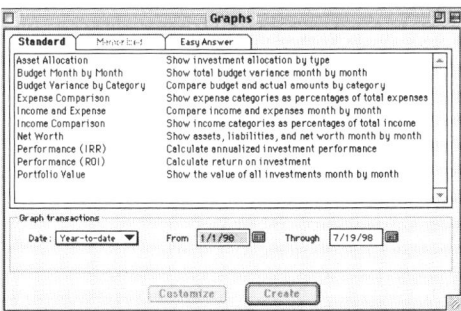

Figure 11.9 Quicken provides a variety of standard reports.

Using a Standard Graph

Standard graphs provide such information as your net worth, the value of your investment portfolio, and details about your income and expenses. You can customize Standard graphs to suit your own needs.

To create a Standard graph:

1. Click the Reporting button in the activity bar.

2. Click the Graphs button in the task bar. The Graphs window appears.

3. Click on the Standard tab. Quicken shows you the Standard graph window (**Figure 11.9**).

4. Select the type of graph that you want to create.

5. If necessary, change the date range of the graph by changing the value of the Date pop-up menu, or by typing in a date or dates in the date fields in the Standard Graphs window.

6. Click the Create button to generate the graph (**Figure 11.10**).

✔ Tip

■ Use QuickZoom with any type of graph to view more detailed information about your finances.

To create a Net Worth graph:

Net Worth graphs are a bit complicated. Your net worth is calculated by subtracting your liabilities from your assets. These bar graphs show your assets above the zero line and your liabilities below the zero line, with your net worth showing as a small red square (hopefully above the zero line!).

1. Click the Reporting button in the Quicken activity bar.

2. Click the Graphs button in the task bar. The Graphs window appears.

3. Click on the Standard tab. Quicken shows you the Standard Graphs window.

4. Select the Net Worth template on the Standard tab.

5. If necessary, change the date range.

6. Click the Create button. Quicken generates your net worth graph (**Figure 11.11**).

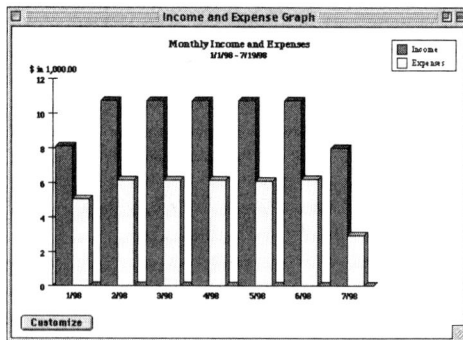

Figure 11.10 You can customize a standard income and expense graph to suit your needs.

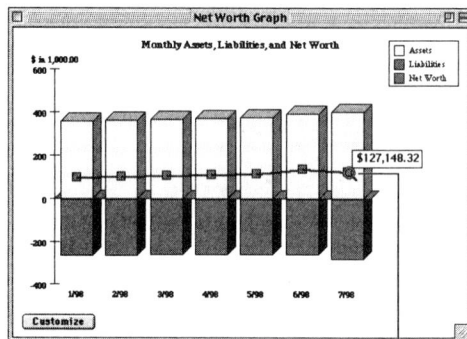

Magnifying glass cursor

Figure 11.11 Hold down the mouse button when the cursor becomes a magnifying glass to see your Net Worth graph, which shows your current net worth dollar value.

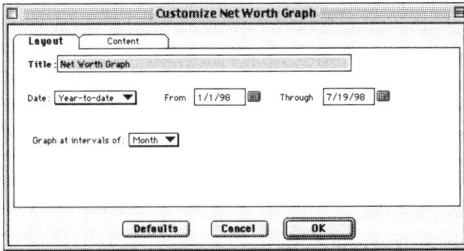

Figure 11.12 You can customize your graphs from this window.

Customizing Graphs

Quicken's standard graph templates are adequate in most cases, but you'll sometimes want to create a custom graph to get some specific information. For example, you might want to compare your income against your spouse's income, or (if you're really looking for marital trouble) compare your expenses.

To create a custom graph:

1. Click the Reporting button on the activity bar, and then click the Graphs button on the task bar.

2. Click on the EasyAnswer or Standard tab in the Graphs window, and then select the kind of graph you wish to create.

3. Click the Customize button. The Customize Graphs window appears (**Figure 11.12**).

4. Click on the Layout tab. If you wish, change the title and date range of the graph.

5. Click on the Content tab. Use the pop-up menus to narrow the scope of the graph.

6. Click the OK button to create your custom graph.

✔ Tips

■ If you have already created a graph, you can customize it by clicking the Customize button in the lower left corner of the Graphs window.

■ If you decide you don't like the changes that you made in the Customize Graphs window, click the Defaults button to return all the settings back to their initial values.

Using Memorized Graphs

Once you have customized a graph, chances are you're going to want to use it again. **Memorized** graphs are customized graphs that you have saved for later reuse.

To memorize a graph:

1. Create a custom graph as described above.

2. Choose Edit > Memorize. The Memorize Graph Template dialog box appears (**Figure 11.13**).

3. Enter a name and a description for the graph. If you click the "Use current date" check box, Quicken will memorize the dates that you specified when you customized the graph.

4. Click the Memorize button.

To use a memorized graph:

1. Click the Graphs button in the task bar.

2. In the Graphs window, click on the Memorized tab (**Figure 11.14**). Select a graph that you previously memorized. Optionally, change the date range at the bottom of the Graphs window to see information pertaining to a particular range.

3. Click the Create button.

To delete a memorized graph:

1. Click the Graphs button in the task bar.

2. In the Graphs window, click on the Memorized tab. Select a graph that you previously memorized.

3. Choose Edit > Delete Graph, or press Command-D.

4. Click the Yes button when Quicken asks you to confirm the deletion.

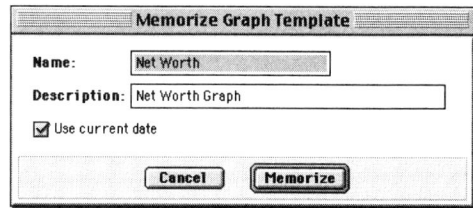

Figure 11.13 After you have customized a graph, you can memorize it and give it a name.

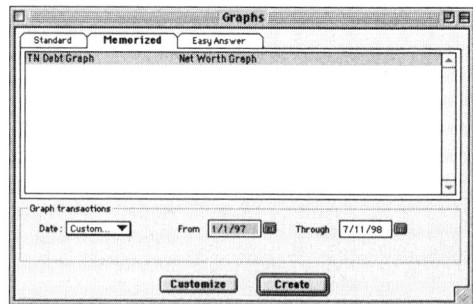

Figure 11.14 Choose a previously memorized report from the Memorized tab.

File
New File...
Open File...
Close Window ⌘W
Page Setup...
Print Preview...
Print Graph...
Print Checks... ⌘P
Import...
Export...
Save a Copy...
Quit ⌘Q

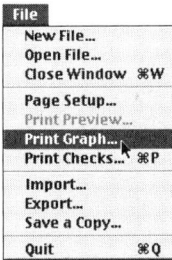

Figure 11.5 You can print any type of Quicken graph simply by choosing Print Graph from the File menu while the graph is displayed on screen.

Printing Graphs

Most of the time, you'll be displaying your graphs onscreen, but on occasion you'll want to print them out to show others. You might want to print an income graph to dazzle a loan officer, for example, or to demonstrate to your doubting parents what a financial whiz you've become.

To print a graph or chart:

1. Open or create a graph or chart.

2. Choose File > Print Graph. The printer dialog box will appear.

3. Click the Print button to print the graph or chart.

PRINTING GRAPHS

WORKING WITH
LOANS AND MORTGAGES

Loans come in two flavors: either you are borrowing money from another person or from a financial institution, or, perhaps a happier sort, you are lending money to someone else. Quicken handles both kinds of loans with aplomb, creating an account for each new loan.

When you are borrowing money, Quicken tracks how the loan is *amortized*, or paid off, to show you the interest you are paying, the remaining principal, and the length and amounts of your payment schedule. When you set up this kind of loan, Quicken automatically creates a *liability* account.

When you loan money to someone else, Quicken sets up a payment schedule and creates an *asset* account.

Creating Loans

To set up a loan account, Quicken needs information about the terms of the loan and the lender or borrower. Then Quicken creates the loan payment schedule and the principal asset or liability account.

To create a loan (when you're the borrower):

1. Click the Assets/Debt button in the Activity bar (**Figure 12.1**)

2. Click the Loans button in the task bar (**Figure 12.2**). The Loans window appears (**Figure 12.3**).

3. Click the New button. The Loan Interview window appears (**Figure 12.4**).

4. Select the radio buttons in the Loan Interview window as appropriate for the loan that you're creating.

5. Click the Continue button to open the Set Up Loan window (**Figure 12.5**).

6. In the Set Up Loan window, enter the name of your lender.

7. Enter the payment amounts. Enter your monthly (or quarterly, annual, etc.) payment in the Principal + Interest field. If you're creating a real estate loan and extra fees are added to the loan, such as PMI, property taxes, etc., enter those amounts too.

8. Enter the date of your first payment.

9. Indicate the frequency of the payment. If this loan will be paid on a schedule other than monthly (the default), change the setting of the Frequency pop-up menu.

10. Enter the total number of payments.

11. Enter the annual interest rate.

Figure 12.1 Click this button to open the Assets/Debt area.

Figure 12.2 Click the Loans button to begin creating a loan.

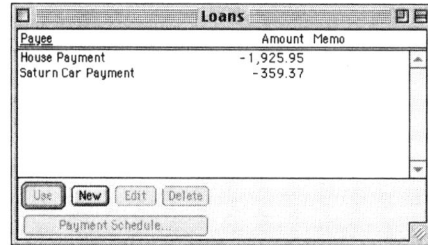

Figure 12.3 The Loans window shows the loans you've entered and lets you start a new loan account.

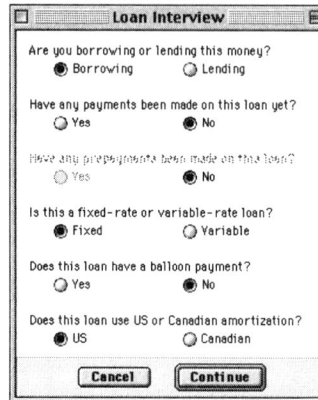

Figure 12.4 Quicken learns about the kind of loan that you want to set up in the Loan Interview window.

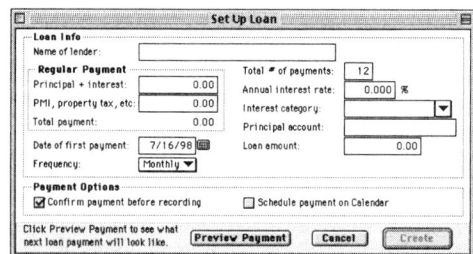

Figure 12.5 You'll enter most of your loan information in the Set Up Loan window.

CREATING LOANS

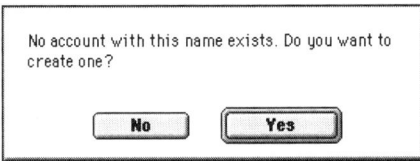

Figure 12.6 Quicken confirms that you want to set up a new liability account.

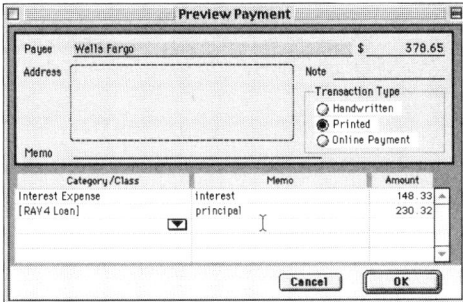

Figure 12.7 The Preview Payment window lets you make sure that your loan is set up correctly before the final creation step occurs.

12. Choose an expense category to track the interest paid on the loan.

13. Enter a name for the principal liability account that you'll use to track this loan. Quicken pops up a dialog box confirming that you want to create a new liability account (**Figure 12.6**).

14. Click the Yes button.

15. Enter the total loan amount.

16. In the Payment Options area, click the "Confirm payment before recording" check box if any of these conditions apply:

• You want to review or change the payment information every time you make a payment.

• You plan to make prepayments to reduce your principal and pay off the loan faster.

• The loan has a variable interest rate.

17. Click the "Schedule payment on Calendar" if you want to be automatically reminded about your loan payment.

18. To make sure that everything looks good before you finish creating the loan, click the Preview Payment button to open the Preview Payment window (**Figure 12.7**).

19. After you've viewed the information, click the OK button to return to the Set Up Loan window.

20. If the loan information looked OK, click the Create button. (If not, make your corections now.)

21. If you clicked the "Schedule payment on Calendar" check box, the Calendar window will open to let you schedule your payment. (See Chapter 7 for information on the Financial Calendar.) Your new loan should appear in the Loans window.

CREATING LOANS

To view your payment schedule:

1. Choose Lists > Loans, or click the Loans button in the task bar, to open the Loans window.

2. In the Loans window, click once on the loan for which you want to see a payment schedule.

3. Click the Payment Schedule button in the Loans window. The Payment Schedule window for that loan appears (**Figure 12.8**).

Wells Fargo Payment Schedule				
Date	Pmt	Principal	Interest	Balance
			8.250%	21,575.98
9/15/98	1	230.32	148.33	21,345.66
10/15/98	2	231.90	146.75	21,113.76
11/15/98	3	233.49	145.16	20,880.27
12/15/98	4	235.10	143.55	20,645.17
1/15/99	5	236.71	141.94	20,408.46
2/15/99	6	238.34	140.31	20,170.12
3/15/99	7	239.98	138.67	19,930.14
4/15/99	8	241.63	137.02	19,688.51
5/15/99	9	243.29	135.36	19,445.22
6/15/99	10	244.96	133.69	19,200.26
7/15/99	11	246.65	132.00	18,953.61
8/15/99	12	248.34	130.31	18,705.27
9/15/99	13	250.05	128.60	18,455.22
10/15/99	14	251.77	126.88	18,203.45
11/15/99	15	253.50	125.15	17,949.95
12/15/99	16	255.24	123.41	17,694.71
1/15/00	17	257.00	121.65	17,437.71

Figure 12.8 You can review the payment schedule for any loan clicking the Payment Schedule button in the Loans window.

✔ Tips

- The term of a loan must be at least 12 months for Quicken to be able to calculate the interest, principal, and payment information.

- For variable-rate loans, you can change the interest rate when you make a payment or whenever your loan's interest rate changes.

- In the Preview Payment window, the principal and interest amount applies to the next scheduled payment only. That's because Quicken calculates the correct amounts of these numbers every time that you make a payment.

- You can specify whether you want to pay your loan with a handwritten check, an online banking transaction, or a printed check by selecting the appropriate radio button in the Preview Payment window.

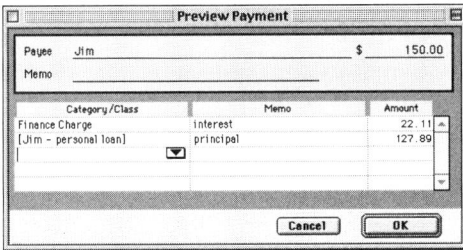

Figure 12.9 When you're the lender, the Preview Payment window is much simpler.

To create a loan (when you're lending):

1. Click the Assets/Debt button in the Activity bar to get to Quicken's Assets/Debt area.

2. Click the Loans button in the task bar. The Loans window appears.

3. Click the New button. The Loan Interview window appears.

4. Select the Lending radio button and any others that are appropriate for this loan and then click the Continue button.

5. Fill out the information in the Set Up Loan window.

6. Click the Preview Payment button. As you can see in **Figure 12.9**, the Preview Payment window is small and uncomplicated when you're the lender.

CREATING A LOAN

Making Loan Payments

To make a loan payment, you first recall the loan payment from the Loans list and enter it in the register of the bank account from which you're making the payment. Quicken then calculates the principal and interest amounts and updates the loan balance.

Of course, you don't have to do this manually if you have a fixed-rate loan. It's easy to schedule the loan payment for automatic entry using the Calendar (as discussed in Chapter 7).

To make a loan payment:

1. Open the account register or the Write Checks window for the bank account from which you'll make the loan payment.

2. Choose Edit > New Transaction, or press Command-N.

3. Choose Lists > Loans. The Loans window appears.

4. Select the loan for which you want to enter a payment and click the Use button, or simply double-click on the loan. The Payment window appears (**Figure 12.10**).

5. If you need to make any adjustments in the Payment window, enter them now. For example, if you have a variable-rate interest loan, you should enter the current interest rate. You can also enter a prepayment if you want to pay off the loan faster.

6. Click the OK button. Quicken will enter the loan payment in the account register.

✔ Tip

■ To see the history of a loan, open the account register for the loan from the Accounts list. Your register should resemble **Figure 12.11**.

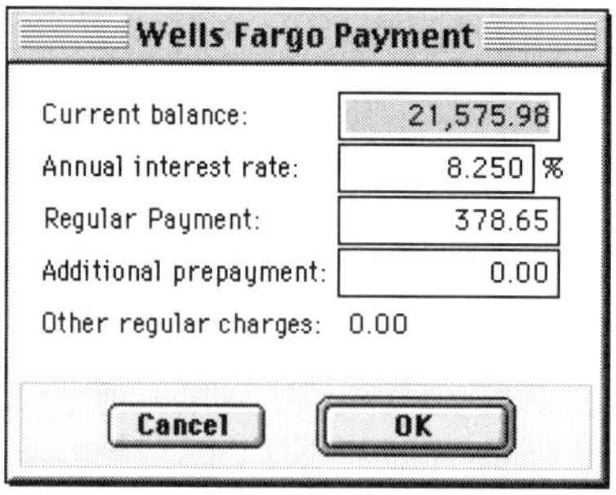

Figure 12.10 You can change the interest rate or add prepayment information in the Loan Payment window.

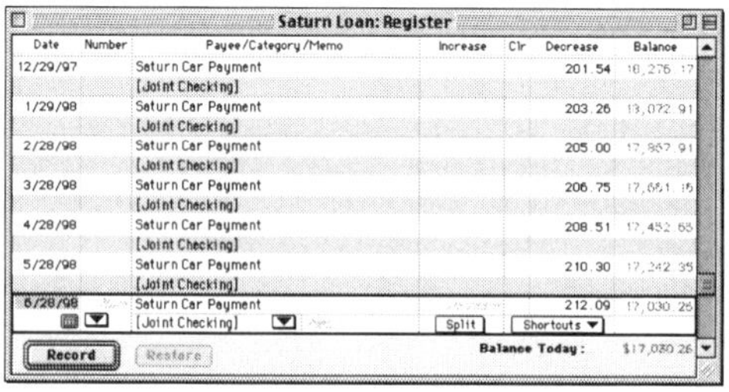

Figure 12.11 You can view the history of your loan at any time by opening the account register for the loan from the Accounts list.

SETTING UP INVESTMENT ACCOUNTS

"Investing? Who needs it? Why, I'm only [fill in some number under 30] years old; I won't need to worry about retirement for a long time."

Sound familiar? When you're in your teens or twenties, retirement is a lifetime away. Ironically, that is just the time that you should begin investing, because you'll have nearly fifty years of compound interest working for you. Professional financial planners like to show how if you save just $100 per month starting when you're 20, you can easily retire with savings of more than a million dollars. But if you wait until you're 30 and make the same investments, you end up with only about a third as much when you're 65.

(If you're already past your twenties and thirties, don't despair—it's never too late to start preparing for your future.)

For the vast majority of us, the key to comfortable living in future years and a successful retirement is a solid savings and investment program. Quicken lets you track the performance of your investments, update current market values, and see whether you're earning or losing money on your investments.

In this chapter, you'll learn how to set up an investment portfolio, how to add investments to your portfolio, and how to set up a mutual fund account in Quicken.

Using Investment Accounts

You can use a variety of account types within Quicken to track your investments. Here are the four choices:

- You can use a regular bank account for investments with a constant share price or no share price. For example, a certificate of deposit earns interest, but the value doesn't go up or down according to a fluctuating market.

- Asset accounts are used to keep track of things that you own, such as personal property, real estate, or other tangible items. For example, if you have a valuable stamp or wine collection, you might track its value in an Asset account so that the collection shows up as part of your net worth. You can update the value of the collection in the Asset account from time to time.

- A portfolio account tracks one or more securities. (A *security* is an investment vehicle, such as a stock, bond, mutual fund, money-market fund, certificate of deposit, precious metal, or collectible.) Your portfolio account can include a mix of securities, and you can use the account to track transactions and provide the total market value for your portfolio. Quicken's many reporting options can show you how your portfolio is performing.

- Each mutual fund account tracks a mutual fund. It's easier to use than the portfolio account if all you want to do is track a single mutual fund. (Of course, you can have as many mutual fund accounts as you wish, each tracking a different mutual fund).

✔ Tip

- One drawback of using a bank account or an asset account is that it cannot track the rate of return on an investment. To track a return rate, you'll need to use a portfolio or money market account.

Table 13.1 If you're not sure which kind of account to use for your investments, take a look at Table 13.1 to see Intuit's recommendations.

Selecting the proper account type for your investment	
INVESTMENT TYPE	ACCOUNT TYPE
Securities for which you want to track a cash balance, such as stocks, bonds, or mutual funds; or a collection of investments in a brokerage account	Portfolio
A single mutual fund with no cash balance	Mutual fund
Money market funds	Bank (if you write checks against the fund) or mutual fund (if you need to track the rate of return)
Certificates of deposit	Bank
Real estate	Asset
IRA accounts, Keogh accounts, variable annuities Unit trusts Real estate investment trusts or partnerships	Portfolio
Treasury bills Fixed annuities, 401(k), 403 (b), pensions Collectibles or precious metals	Portfolio or asset

Setting up Your Portfolio

Before you get started setting up your portfolio accounts, you need to decide how much investment history you want to include in your records. You have three options: a complete history, just this year's information, or what I call the "Aw-the-heck-with-it" method —just enter your current investment holdings. (For a detailed rundown of the pros and cons of each method, see the Quicken User Guide.)

If you choose the complete history option, you'll need to enter the initial purchase price for each security and all subsequent transactions. On the plus side, all your reports are complete, and Quicken can accurately calculate capital gains. On the minus side, if you been investing for several years, that's a lot of data to enter. However, Intuit recommends this option, and so do I.

If you decide to enter just this year's data, you'll enter the investment balances as of the end of last year and then enter all of the transactions for each security since the beginning of this year. With this method, the information you need to find and enter is more recent and probably easier for you to obtain. Reports that deal with events from this year will be accurate, and if you sell a security, Quicken will be able to track which lots of that security you should sell to minimize or maximize your short-term capital gains. This method's disadvantage is that Quicken will not know the original cost of the security (called the *cost basis*), so you can't get accurate long-term capital gains or realized gain reports.

The "Aw-the-heck-with-it" method is the fastest, and reports that cover events after today will be accurate. You just enter in your current investment holdings. On the other hand, data for this year and past years will be incomplete, and you won't be able to get reports for capital gains or realized gains.

Figure 13.1 Click the Investing button to open Quicken's investment area.

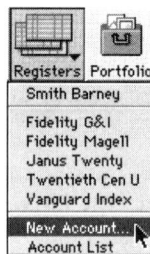

Figure 13.2 Click the Registers button to open a pop-up menu to set up a new account.

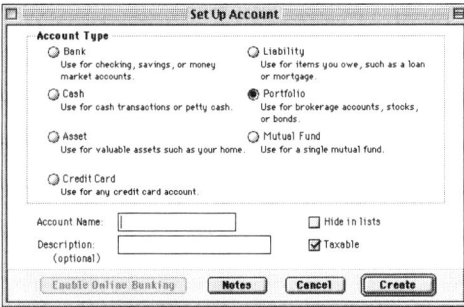

Figure 13.3 You can create a new portfolio from the Set Up Account window.

Figure 13.4 When you set up a new portfolio account, Quicken opens an associated account register.

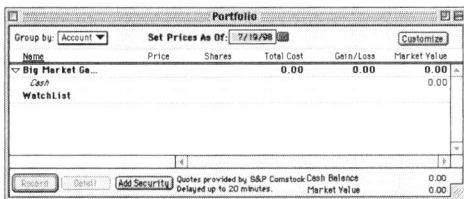

Figure 13.5 The Portfolio window shows all of your investment accounts.

Figure 13.6 To add a security to your portfolio, enter its name.

To create a portfolio account:

1. Click the Investing button in the activity bar (**Figure 13.1**).

2. Click the Registers button in the task bar, and then choose New Account (**Figure 13.2**). The Set Up Account window appears (**Figure 13.3**).

3. Select the Portfolio radio button.

4. Enter the name of the portfolio account in the Account Name box.

5. In the Description box, add a short description of the account (optional).

6. If the account is taxable, make sure that the Taxable box is checked. If this account is going to be tax-free, clear the Taxable box.

7. Click the Create button. Quicken opens a new account register for the new portfolio account (**Figure 13.4**).

To add securities to your portfolio:

1. Click the Portfolio button at the bottom of the new account register. The Portfolio window will appear (**Figure 13.5**), containing the account you just created.

   If you had previously created other investment accounts, they would appear in the Portfolio window as well. All investment accounts are listed in a single Portfolio window.

2. Click the Add Security button at the bottom of the Portfolio window. The Security Name dialog box appears (**Figure 13.6**).

3. Type in a name for the new security, and then click the OK button.

CREATE A PORTFOLIO ACCOUNT

107

4. Quicken pops up a dialog box that says it can't find that security (**Figure 13.7**). Click the Set Up button. The Set Up Security window appears (**Figure 13.8**).

5. In the Symbol box, enter the stock ticker symbol for the security.

6. In the Type box, choose one of the options from the pop-up menu (Bond, CD, Mutual fund, or Stock).

7. In the Goal box, choose one of the options from the pop-up menu (College fund, Growth, High-risk, Income, or Low-risk).

8. Ignore the "Notify if price is" boxes.

9. If the security is taxable, make sure the "Taxable" box is checked. Make sure that the "Hide in lists" box is not checked.

10. Click the Create button. The Add Security dialog appears (**Figure 13.9**).

11. If you own the security, select the "Add shares to account" radio button and click OK. The Action Type List window appears.

or

If you don't own the security but want to track its performance, select "Add security to WatchList." Then click OK.

You can add securities that interest you but that you don't yet own in the WatchList area to track how they do. If you choose this option, setup for that security is complete.

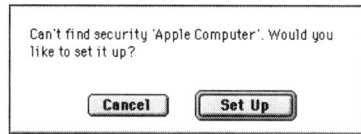

Figure 13.7 Click the Set Up button to reassure Quicken that you want to create a new security.

Figure 13.8 Use the Set Up Security window to enter details of the new security.

Figure 13.9 Select an option from the Add Security dialog to tell Quicken that you own the security or that you're just keeping an eye on it.

Figure 13.10 You must indicate that you acquired the security before you began using Quicken or that you'll be transferring funds from another Quicken account to purchase the security.

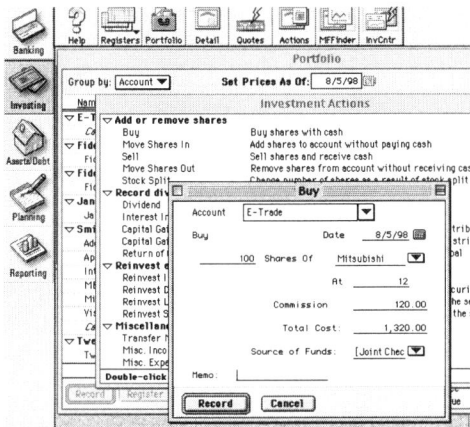

Figure 13.11 When you buy stocks, you always want to keep track of the purchase price and commission so that later, when you sell them, you can gauge your profit (or loss). Here you also note the source of funds with which you bought your shares.

12. If you selected the "Add shares to account" radio button in step 11, the Action Type dialog box (**Figure 13.10**) appears. You must tell Quicken whether you acquired the security before or after you started using Quicken. Select "Move shares in" to add shares that you already owned to the portfolio account without using funds from any Quicken account to purchase those shares. Click OK and the Move Shares In window appears.

or

Select the "Buy" radio button to purchase shares with funds from another Quicken account. Click the OK button to open the Buy dialog box, and then go to step 15.

13. In the Move Shares In window, enter the date, the number of shares in the security that you own, the price you bought the shares for, and a memo (optional).

14. Click the Record button. The security shows up in the Portfolio window

15. If you selected "Buy" in step 12, the Buy dialog box appears (**Figure 13.11**). Fill in the date, the number of shares, the price you bought the shares for, the broker commission (if any), and the source of funds (must be another Quicken account). Click the Record button and the security will show up in the Portfolio window.

✔ Tips

■ If you leave the Source of Funds field blank when purchasing a security, Quicken deducts the money for it from the Portfolio account.

■ If you leave the Destination of Funds field blank when selling a security, Quicken credits the proceeds of the sale to the Portfolio account.

ADD SECURITIES TO YOUR PORTFOLIO

To add a mutual fund to your portfolio:

1. Click the Investing button in the activity bar.

2. Click the Registers button in the task bar, and then choose New Account. The Set Up Account window appears (as shown in **Figure 13.3**).

3. Select the Mutual Fund radio button.

4. Enter the name of the mutual fund in the Account Name box.

5. In the Description box, add a short description of the mutual fund (optional).

6. If the mutual fund is taxable, make sure that the "Taxable" box is checked. If this is a tax-free fund, clear the "Taxable" box.

7. Click the Create button. Quicken opens an account register for the new mutual fund account (**Figure 13.12**).

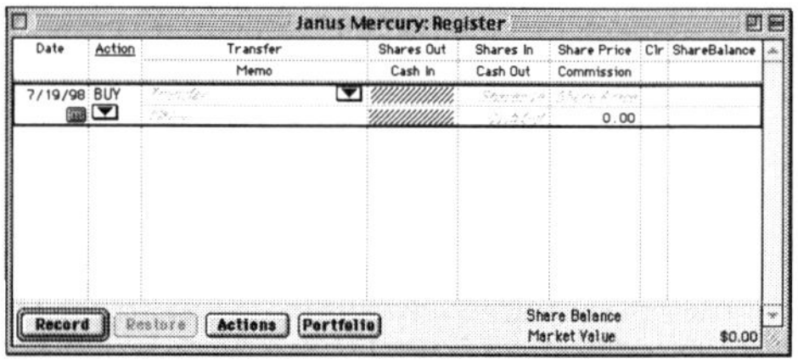

Figure 13.12 Quicken maintains an account register for mutual funds, as with every other kind of account.

MANAGING
YOUR INVESTMENTS

After setting up your investment portfolio (see Chapter 13), you need to manage your investments on an ongoing basis. That means updating the share prices of your securities and making entries whenever you buy or sell an investment.

Getting up-to-date quotes on stocks, bonds, and mutual funds is easy if you have access to the Internet or use CompuServe. If you have a modem and access to the Internet or CompuServe, Quicken can download securities prices and enter them directly into your Portfolio window.

Quicken also allows you to view and manually enter security prices in either the Portfolio window or the Security Detail window.

To manually update prices in the Portfolio window:

1. Click the Investing button in the activity bar (**Figure 14.1**).

2. Click the Portfolio button in the task bar (**Figure 14.2**). The Portfolio window appears (**Figure 14.3**).

3. At the top of the Portfolio window, you'll see a date next to "Set Prices As Of." If you're updating securities prices as of another day (the default is today's date), change this date.

4. Select a security in the Portfolio window by clicking on it, and then enter a share price for the displayed date by clicking at the appropriate spot in the Price column, as shown in **Figure 14.3**. You can enter a price either as a decimal number or as a fraction.

5. Click the Record button (or press the Return or Enter key) to save the new price. Quicken will recalculate the value of that security and your whole portfolio.

✔ Tips

■ In the Price column, you can increase or decrease the price by $1/8$ share (0.125) by pressing the plus (+) or hyphen (-) key.

■ If the prices in the Portfolio window appear to be incorrect, press Command-Option-U to force a recalculation of your entire Portfolio.

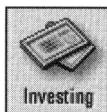

Figure 14.1 Click the Investing button to switch to Quicken's investment area.

Figure 14.2 Click the Portfolio button to open the Portfolio window.

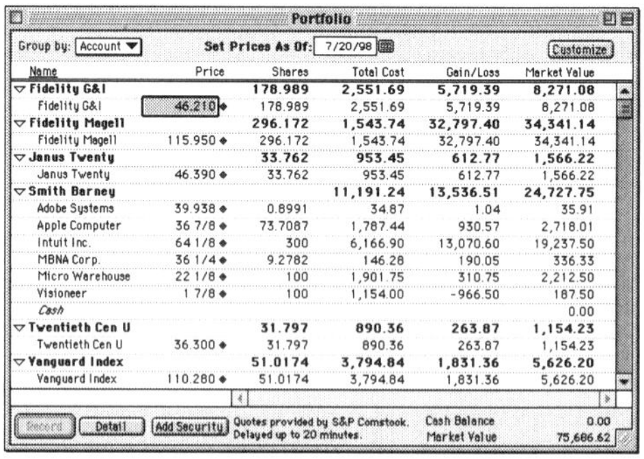

Figure 14.3 You can use the Portfolio window to view all of your investments.

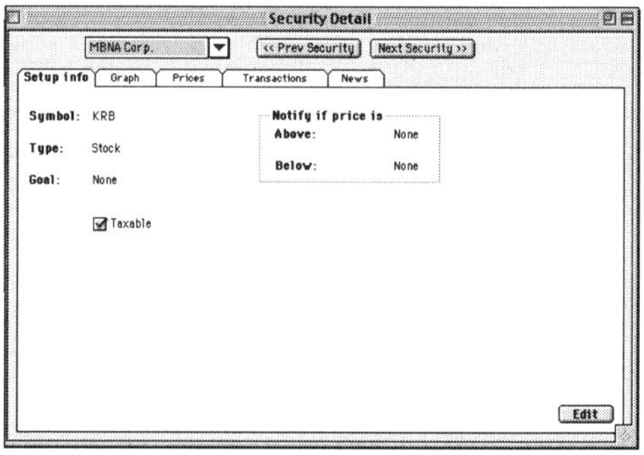

Figure 14.4 The Security Detail window provides a wealth of information about a security.

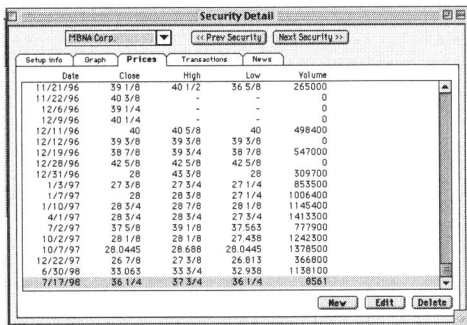

Figure 14.5 You can view the price history of the security from the Prices tab of the Security Detail window.

Figure 14.6 You can change a stock price in the New Price dialog.

To manually update prices in the Security Detail window:

1. In the Portfolio window, double-click on a security name, or click the Detail button at the bottom of the window. A Security Detail window will appear (**Figure 14.4**).

2. Click on the Prices tab (**Figure 14.5**).

3. Make necessary changes to the prices:

• To enter a new price, click the New button and fill out the New Price dialog (**Figure 14.6**); then click the Record button.

• To change a price, click the Edit button, fill out the Edit Price dialog (which looks almost identical to the New Price dialog), and then click the Change button.

• To delete a price, select the price that you wish to delete and click the Delete button. Quicken will ask you to confirm the deletion. Choose OK to confirm.

MANUALLY UPDATEING PRICES

To set up Quicken to download price quotes:

1. Choose Edit > Preferences, and then click the Quotes icon in the scrolling area on the left (**Figure 14.7**).

2. Select the source for your online quotes:

- The "900 service" is the Quicken Quotes Hotline. It costs $1 per minute. The Hotline number is preset.

- If you're already a member of the CompuServe online service, you can select "Use CompuServe" and then enter your account number and password.

- Most people will select "Use Internet." If you have access to the Internet via America Online, CompuServe, or another Internet Service Provider, you can get free quotes from the Quicken Financial Network on the Web.

- The Investor Insight service is no longer in operation, so don't bother choosing this one. It was replaced in July 1998 by the Quicken Financial Network.

3. Click the Modem icon in the scrolling area on the left to open the Modem Preferences window.(**Figure 14.8**).

4. Click the Autoconfigure button to have Quicken set up your modem automatically.

5. Click the OK button to save your settings.

✔ Tip

- In rare cases, Autoconfigure will be unable to set up your modem. If this happens, consult the Quicken User Manual to identify the problem.

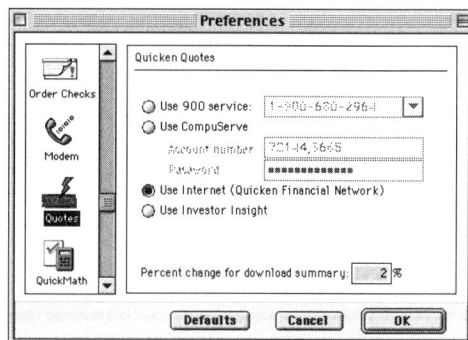

Figure 14.7 You can choose an online service to download your stock quotes from the Preferences window.

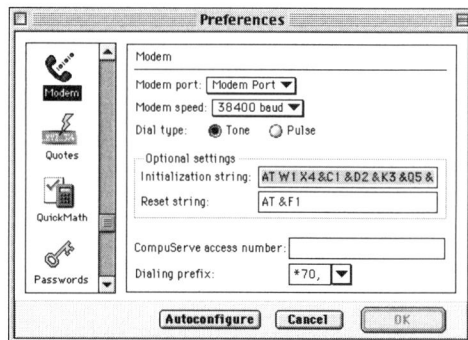

Figure 14.8 You can adjust your modem settings in the Modem Preferences window.

Figure 14.9 Click the Quotes button to download security quotes.

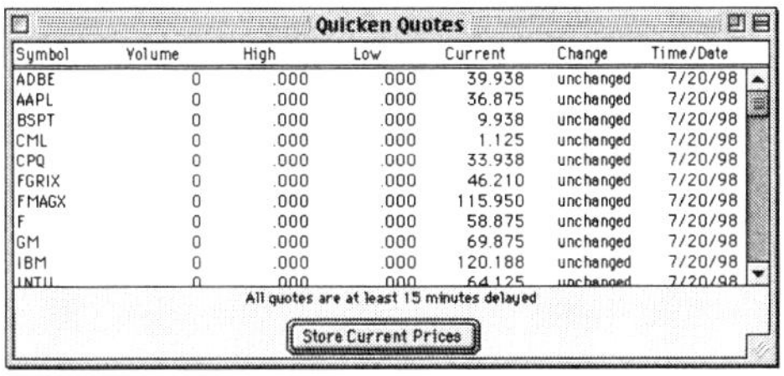

Figure 14.10 Click the Store Current Prices button in the Quicken Quotes window to save the updated prices in your portfolio.

To download price quotes:

1. Click the Investing button in the activity bar.

2. Click the Quotes button in the task bar (**Figure 14.9**). Quicken will connect to the online service you specified in Preferences and download the latest prices of your securities.

3. Quicken then opens a Quicken Quotes window showing you the downloaded price information for every security in your Portfolio (**Figure 14.10**).

4. Click the Store Current Prices button to have Quicken enter the prices in your portfolio.

✔ Tips

■ You can download prices as many times per day you wish, but Quicken stores only one price per day. Every time you click the Store Current Prices button, Quicken replaces the prices in your Portfolio with the most recent price.

■ The stock symbols in your setup must be exactly the same as those used by the markets. If the message "Ticker not found" appears in your Quicken Quotes window, check to make sure that your stock symbols are correct.

■ Stocks, options, and indexes are updated constantly during the business day, although the quotes you get online are delayed by about 20 minutes. Prices for mutual funds are updated only once per day at 6 p.m. Eastern time.

DOWNLOAD PRICE QUOTES

115

Buying and Selling Securities

Most of the transactions in your investment accounts will involve buying or selling securities, but Quicken can handle virtually any sort of investment transaction. Table 14.1 shows the transactions available in Quicken. The investment process is so complex that I don't have room to explain it all here. Refer to the Quicken User Manual to learn about complex investment transactions.

You can enter investment transactions by two methods: by using investment forms or by entering information directly into the investment account register. The investment forms are easier to use, especially if you're new to these sorts of transactions. After you become familiar with investment transactions, you may choose to use the other entry method, which is to simply enter the information into the investment account register.

Table 14.1

Investment actions	
ACTION	DESCRIPTION
Buy	Buy security with cash
Capital Gain Long	Receive cash from long-term capital gains distribution
Capital Gain Short	Receive cash from short-term capital gains distribution
Dividend	Receive cash from dividend
Interest Income	Receive cash from interest income
Miscellaneous Expense	Pay miscellaneous expense with cash
Miscellaneous Income	Receive cash from miscellaneous income
Move Shares In	Add shares to account
Move Shares Out	Remove shares from account
Reinvest Dividend	Reinvest in shares of the security with money from dividend or income distribution
Reinvest Interest	Reinvest in shares of the security with money from interest distribution
Reinvest Long	Reinvest in shares of the security with money from long-term capital gains distribution
Reinvest Short	Reinvest in shares of the security with money from short-term capital gains distribution
Return of Capital	Receive cash from return of capital
Sell	Sell security and receive cash
Stock Split	Change number of shares as result of stock split
Transfer Money	Transfer money into or out of this account

Figure 14.11 Begin an investment transaction by clicking the Actions button in the task bar.

Figure 14.12 Choose the kind of investment transaction you want in the Investment Actions window.

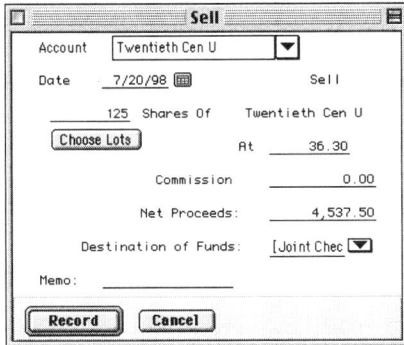

Figure 14.13 Fill out the investment detail window to complete your transaction.

To use investment forms for transactions:

1. Click the Investing button in the activity bar.

2. Click the Portfolio button in the task bar to open the Portfolio window.

3. Click on a security to select it in the Portfolio window.

4. Click the Actions button in the task bar (**Figure 14.11**). The Investment Actions window appears (**Figure 14.12**).

5. Find the transaction that you wish to perform in the Investment Actions window, and double-click it. The detail window for the transaction you choose will open (**Figure 14.13**). (In this case, Sell was chosen in the Investment Actions window.)

6. Fill out the information in the detail window, and then click the Record button.

USING INVESTMENT FORMS FOR TRANSACTIONS

PLANNING FOR THE FUTURE

One of the things I like about Quicken is its ability to shed light on the past, present, and future of my financial life. I can use it to look back to where I've been, to deal with my current finances, and to help me create my future financial scenario.

Sometimes I just want to look a little way into the future, so I use the Financial Calendar to see which payments are scheduled for next month. If my finances were a bit more predictable (that they aren't is a side effect of my life as a freelance writer), I might be interested in creating a yearly budget. However, I do plan to retire someday, so I use Quicken's retirement planners to see whether I'm on track with my savings and investment programs.

Quicken Deluxe 98 includes several tools under the Financial Fitness banner that can help you now as well as in the future, including the Debt Reduction Planner, the Retirement Planner, and the Tax Deduction Finder.

In this chapter you'll learn how to use the Financial Fitness planners and some of Quicken's other tools that can help you take control of your finances now and plan for your future financial well-being.

Using the Financial Fitness Planners

Quicken Deluxe 98 includes six programs under the Financial Fitness banner. These programs walk you through the process of creating financial plans to meet your specific goals. After asking you a series of questions and drawing on the numbers in your Quicken data file, the programs create a financial action plan for you.

To make your work easier, the Financial Fitness planners include audio and QuickTime movies that show examples and illustrate financial concepts. To hear the sounds and view the movies, the Quicken Deluxe CD must be in your CD-ROM drive. You can also run the Financial Fitness programs without the CD (but you'll miss the multimedia treats).

Here's a rundown of Quicken's six Financial Fitness planners:

Net Worth Analysis gives you a snapshot of your current financial picture by asking you questions about what you own and what you owe. This planner is a useful starting point.

Many people are carrying too large a load of consumer debt, and the **Debt Reduction Planner** will show you how to get out of debt faster and save money while doing it. If you follow the recommendations in this planner, you can save hundreds or even thousands of dollars in interest payments.

The **Retirement Planner** probes your savings and investment plans and tells you whether or not your current plan (if you have one) is adequate to meet your needs when you retire. If not, the planner will come up with a new plan to help you meet your goals.

Financial Fitness Limitations

Although the Financial Fitness tools give you valuable information and viable action plans, you shouldn't rely on them as your sole source for financial planning.

The reason for this is simple: the world has changed in the short time since these programs were written. For example, the Tax Deduction Finder is based on 1997 tax year information and the tax law has changed since then. Other programs, such as the Retirement Planner, contain assumptions that could no longer be completely accurate or don't take into account new financial instruments, such as the Roth IRA, which is a new kind of Individual Retirement Account that can provide significant savings for some people.

The Financial Fitness planners are a good guide, but don't take them as gospel. And before you make any big financial moves, it's always a good idea to consult your accountant or financial planner.

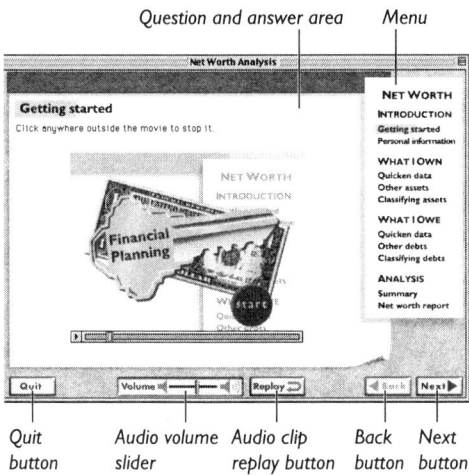

Figure 15.1 You can choose a topic or watch a movie from the "Getting started" screen of any of the Financial Fitness planners.

The **Emergency Records Organizer** helps you gather and track important financial and legal documents.

The less tax you pay, the better your bottom line, and the **Tax Deduction Finder** helps you determine whether you're eligible for certain tax deductions.

The final Financial Fitness tool is a **Free Credit Report** that you can request from one of the major credit reporting agencies. The report will be delivered to your home address within four to six weeks. You can also pay a fee for faster delivery.

Each of these programs work in much the same way. Each planner displays a menu on the right side of the screen that shows the topics the planner covers (**Figure 15.1**). You can jump to any topic by clicking it, but it's usually best to work through the planner sequentially.

The main part of the planner screen is the question and answer area, where you'll see QuickTime movies and answer questions about your finances. It's also where you'll enter financial data. At the end of the process, Quicken will generate and show you an action plan that you can print out and use.

Control buttons along the bottom of each planner screen let you quit the planner, control the audio volume, replay movies and sound clips, and move sequentially through the planner.

Because each planner is used in a similar way, I'll go into only two of them in detail here: the Debt Reduction Planner and the Emergency Records Organizer.

USING THE FINANCIAL FITNESS PLANNERS

Reducing Consumer Debt

Paying off your credit card and loan debts is an important step toward financial happiness. If you don't pay off your credit card and loan bills in full every month, you are charged interest to compensate the bank for your use of their money. Unfortunately, interest payments aren't a good deal for you; the money that you pay in interest is unproductive and could be spent in better ways.

Quicken's Debt Reduction Planner uses a simple philosophy. It analyzes your debt and pays off the highest interest rate cards first, which lets you get out of debt faster while paying less interest.

To use the Debt Reduction Planner:

1. Click the Assets/Debt button in the activity bar (**Figure 15.2**).

2. Click the Debt Plan button in the task bar (**Figure 15.3**). The Debt Reduction Planner "Getting started" screen appears (**Figure 15.4**).

3. If the Quicken Deluxe CD is in your machine's CD-ROM drive, Quicken will play a brief movie explaining the purpose and methods used by the Debt Reduction Planner. Without the CD, you'll go straight to work. Click a check box next to a question to get information about reducing debt.

4. Click the Next button. The "Personal information" screen appears (**Figure 15.5**).

Figure 15.2 Click the Assets/Debt button to switch to Quicken's debt planning area.

Figure 15.3 Click the Debt Plan button to open the Debt Reduction Planner.

Figure 15.4 You can ask questions about reducing your debt in the "Getting started" screen.

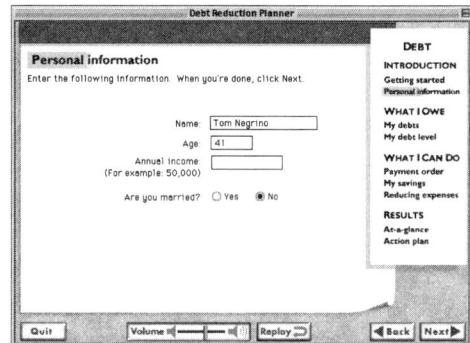

Figure 15.5 Tell the planner a little about yourself in this screen.

Figure 15.6 The "What I owe" screen explains how you tell the planner about your debts.

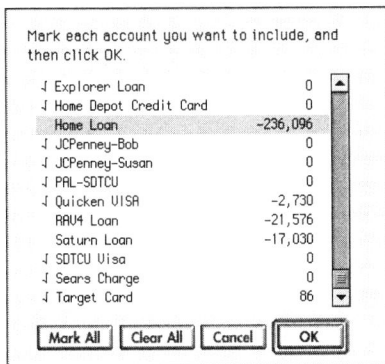

Figure 15.7 Mark or unmark your debts to include them in the planner.

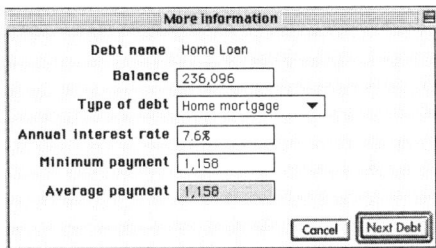

Figure 15.8 In this screen, you tell the planner about the terms of each debt.

5. Fill out your personal information, and then click the Next button to go to the next section. The next screen (**Figure 15.6**) explains what you'll do in this section, called "What I owe." Click the Next button.

6. The planner consults your Quicken data file, gathers all of your debts, and displays them in a scrolling list (**Figure 15.7**). Initially, all of the debts are marked with checkmarks; click on a debt to unmark it if it has a zero balance or if you don't want to include it in the debt reduction plan. Click the OK button.

7. In the "More information" screen (**Figure 15.8**), you'll tell the planner detailed information about each debt. The planner already knows the balance owed on each debt. In the "Type of debt" pop-up menu, choose "Consumer debt," "Home mortgage," or "Other debt."

8. Enter the annual interest rate for the loan or credit card.

9. Enter the minimum monthly payment.

10. Enter the average monthly payment that you actually make, if it's different from the minimum payment. You don't need to be too picky about this figure; just get it in the ballpark. Click the Next Debt button.

11. Repeat steps 7 through 10 for each of your debts that has a balance. Naturally, if a credit card has a zero balance, you don't need to worry about including it in a repayment plan. When you get through all of the "More information" screens, click the Next button.

REDUCING CONSUMER DEBT

12. The planner calculates your debt situation and displays the "My debt level" screen (**Figure 15.9**). This screen tells you when you can expect to pay off your debts if you make no changes to your payment plans and rates your consumer debt level as low, medium, or high. Click the Next button to move to the next section, where you'll begin formulating your action plan to get out of debt sooner.

Figure 15.9 The "My debt level" screen shows you just how high your consumer debt level really is.

13. The "What I can do" section begins with a screen that outlines the steps you'll take next (**Figure 15.10**). Read this information, and then click Next.

14. The "Payment order" screen (**Figure 15.11**) shows you the planner's suggested order of paying off your debts, based on the interest rate for each debt, with higher rates listed first. If you want to reorder the debts for some reason (for example, because you prefer to pay off one debt before another), you can drag debts up or down in the list. Click the Optimize button at the bottom of the list to return to the list's most cost-effective order. After the debts are in order, click the Next button.

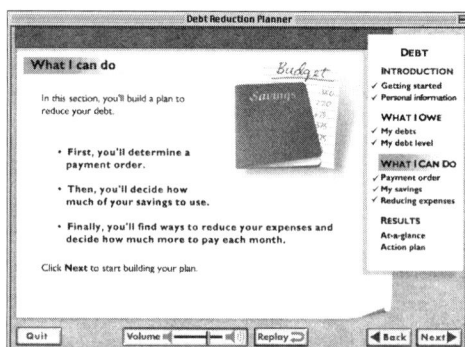

Figure 15.10 In the "What I can do" section, you'll begin steps to create your debt reduction plan.

15. The planner taps into your Quicken data file once again to check the values of your bank, cash, and investment accounts (**Figure 15.12**). You should enter an amount you're willing to pay to immediately reduce your debt. (See the "Spending Savings to Reduce Debt" sidebar for more information.) Click the Next button.

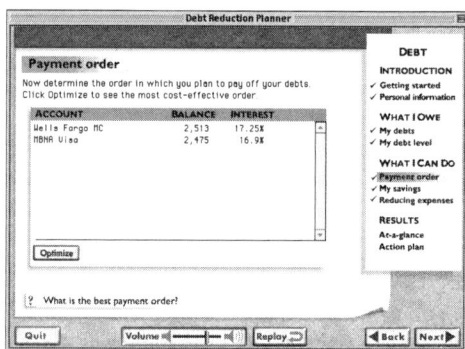

Figure 15.11 Drag debts up and down in the list to set the payment order for your debts.

Figure 15.12 Decide how much of your savings you want to use to reduce your debt in this screen.

Figure 15.13 The "Reducing expenses" screen lets you budget an additional amount per month toward paying debts.

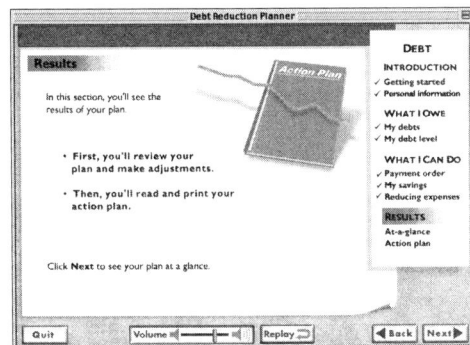

Figure 15.14 Read the "Results" introduction screen to see what comes next.

16. If you can squeeze just a bit out of your monthly budget and throw that money at bills, money will often "come back" to you in the form of savings on interest payments. In the "Reducing expenses" screen (**Figure 15.13**), enter how much more you're willing to pay toward your debt each month. Click Next.

17. In the "Results" section (yes, you're almost done), you can review your action plan and print it out for later reference (**Figure 15.14**). Click Next.

Spending Savings to Reduce Debt

If you already have some money saved, you might question the wisdom of taking money out of your savings or investment accounts to help pay off your consumer debt. Although it is a smart idea to have a financial cushion, you need to ask yourself if your money is working for you in the best way.

For example, assume that you have $2,000 in an investment that is earning 10 percent interest, but your credit cards are charging you 16 percent interest. At the end of the year, you'll have lost money by not paying off your credit cards. You're better off reducing your debt as quickly as possible.

18. The "At-a-glance" screen (**Figure 15.15**) tells you the results of your plan, including how much you'll save in interest and how much sooner you'll pay off your debt. If you want to see the effects of using more savings or paying even more per month, enter that information here and then click the Recalculate button. When you're done, click the Next button.

19. The "Action plan" screen gives you the entire lowdown of your debt reduction plan (**Figure 15.16**). Scroll through and review the plan, and then click the Print button to print a hard copy for easy reference.

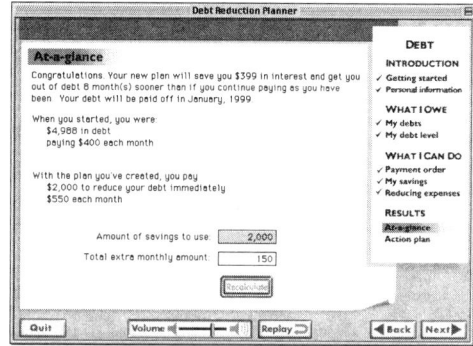

Figure 15.15 To see the effects of paying even more per month, enter the amount in this screen and click the Recalculate button.

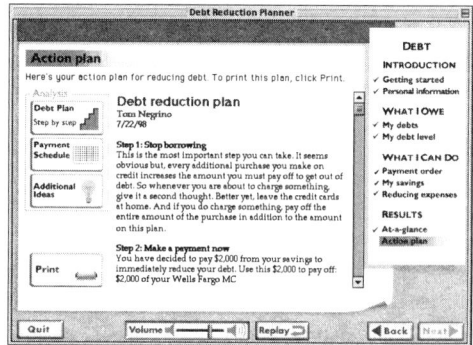

Figure 15.16 Click the Print button to print your debt reduction action plan.

Getting Organized

So many documents in our lives are important, yet most of us don't bother to keep them in one place, ready for easy access in the event that we or a family member will need them.

The Emergency Records Organizer helps you bring together all of the information that you, your family, or your friends would need in an emergency, such as medical insurance information, medical contacts, bank accounts, and even wills or other legal documents.

Because each section in the Emergency Records Organizer works in a similar fashion, I'm going to discuss the planner's highlights rather than take you through every possible step.

To use the Emergency Records Organizer:

1. In Quicken, Choose Activities > Financial Fitness > Emergency Records Organizer. The Organizer's "Getting started" screen appears (**Figure 15.17**).

2. Click on a question to view a QuickTime movie about that question. When you're done asking questions, click the Next button to open the "Security" screen (**Figure 15.18**).

3. If you want to protect your emergency records file from prying eyes, enter a password, and then enter it again for verification. Click Next to get to the "Personal Information" screen (**Figure 15.19**).

4. Fill in your name, address, telephone number, date of birth, and Social Security number. Then click the "Add more info" button. The "More Personal Information" screen appears (**Figure 15.20**).

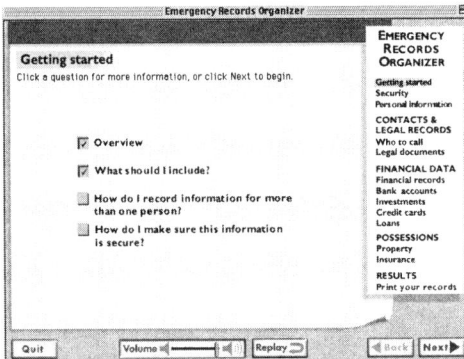

Figure 15.17 You can ask Quicken these questions before you get started.

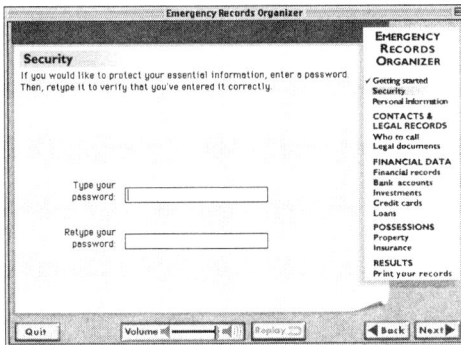

Figure 15.18 To protect your essential information from others who may be using your computer, type in a password.

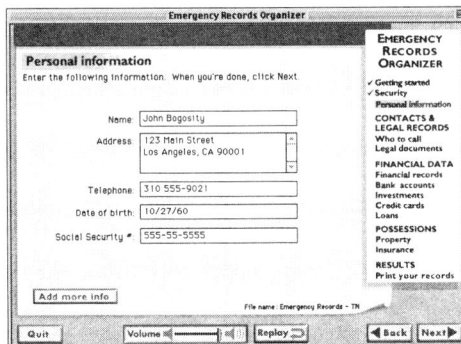

Figure 15.19 Enter your name, address, telephone number, and other personal information here.

GETTING ORGANIZED

5. Fill in your driver's license number, your mother's maiden name, and other ID information, such as the license numbers of any professional licenses you hold. Also include any vital medical warnings, such as allergies. Click OK to return to the "Personal information" screen.

6. Click the Next button to enter the "Contracts & legal records" area. Read the information explaining what's in this section, and then click the Next button to get to the "Who to call" screen (**Figure 15.21**).

7. Under the Contacts heading, choose one of the contact categories. An entry screen will appear in the middle of the window (**Figure 15.22**), where you can type in information about your contacts.

8. Fill in the information in the entry screen, and then click the New button if you want to add more people in that category. Click on another category of Contacts to add information to that category. When you're done adding contacts, click the Next button to get to the "Legal documents" area (**Figure 15.23**).

9. Choose one of the Document types to begin filling out a form describing that document. Repeat as necessary for all of the document types you wish to enter.

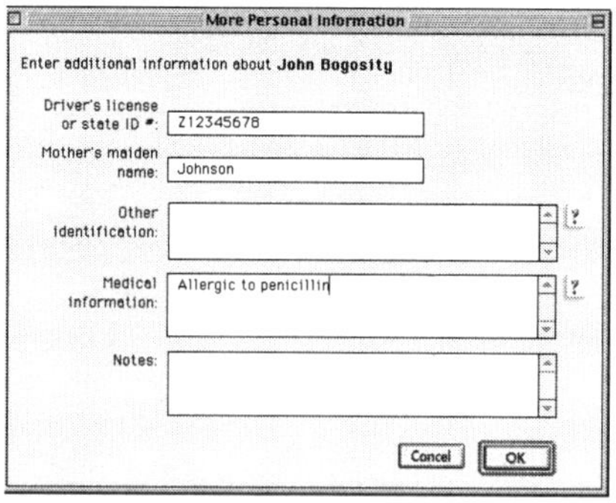

Figure 15.20 Fill in additional personal information in this screen.

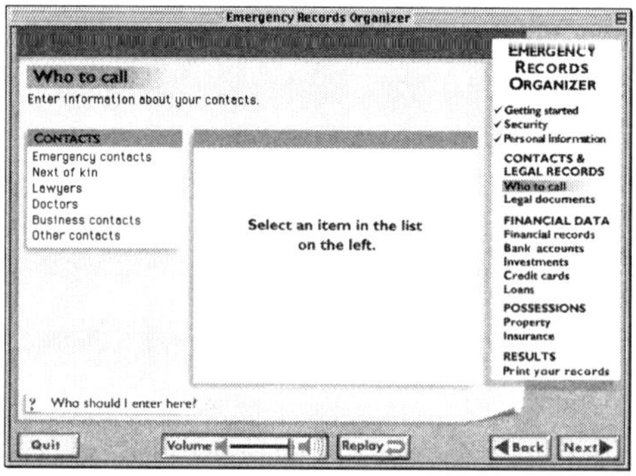

Figure 15.21 Indicate the type of contacts you want to enter.

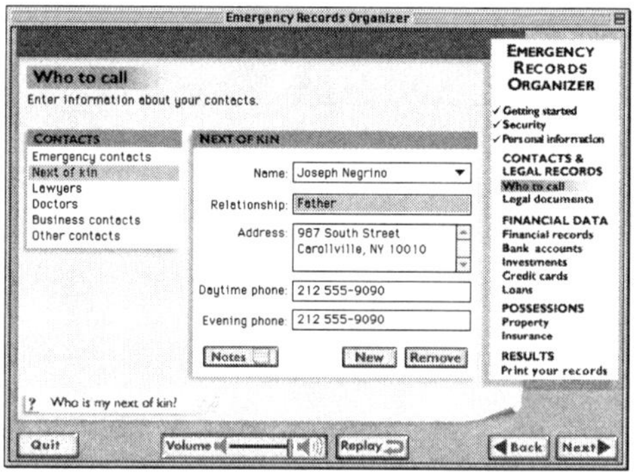

Figure 15.22 After you indicate the contact category, enter each contact's name in this screen.

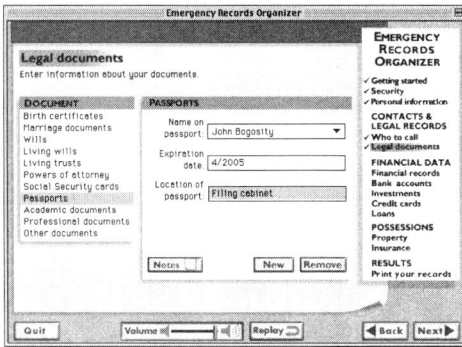

Figure 15.23 Organize and keep track of all your important documents in this screen.

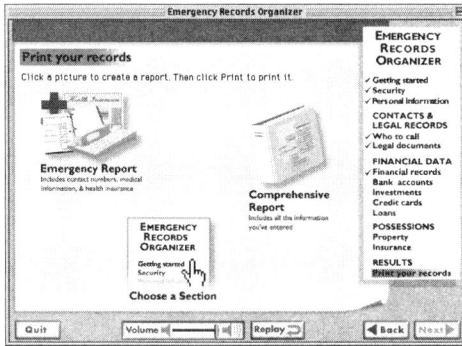

Figure 15.24 You can print three kinds of reports.

10. Repeat the entry steps above for all of the Financial Data and Possessions sections in which you want to enter data. When you're done, click "Print your records" in the menu on the right side of the screen. The "Print your records" screen appears (**Figure 15.24**).

11. Click an icon to choose what type of report you want to print:

- The Emergency Report prints contact numbers, medical history, and insurance information.

- The Comprehensive Report prints all of the information you entered.

- Click Choose a Section to pick the sections of the Organizer that you want to print.

A preview dialog box will open, showing you how the report will look when printed.

Click the Print button to print your report.

Using the Financial Calculators

Quicken (both the Basic and Deluxe versions) includes five financial planning calculators to let you try "what if?" scenarios. You can use these calculators to get quick answers when you're considering a financial move, such as taking on a new mortgage. The financial planning calculators all work in basically the same way—except that the information you enter and the calculations Quicken makes will be different.

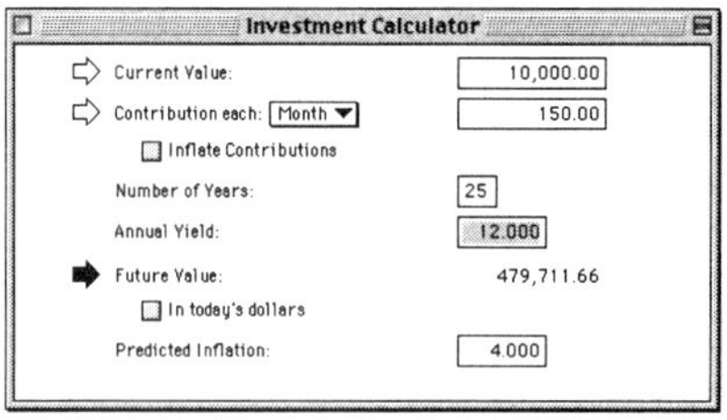

Figure 15.25 Use the financial planning calculator for quick "what-if?" analyses.

To use a financial calculator:

1. Choose Activities > Planning Calculators, and then choose the calculator that you want from the five in the menu. The calculator screen opens (**Figure 15.25**).

2. Click the arrow next to the type of calculation that you want Quicken to figure out.

3. Enter information into the calculator, and Quicken displays the results.

QUICKEN AT TAX TIME

Personally, I don't know anyone who enjoys paying taxes. I've heard that such people actually exist, but I've never met them. For the rest of us, preparing and paying taxes is a yearly ritual that we could easily live without.

Quicken can help to ease some of the pain (although if you end up writing a check instead of receiving a refund, Quicken can't do anything about the agony you'll feel). By properly categorizing your income and expenses throughout the year, you'll be able to create reports that make filling out your tax forms much easier. Using these reports can also save you money if your taxes are prepared by someone else, because the preparer will have less digging to do to get a clear picture of your financial situation.

If you're the do-it-yourself type, you can export Quicken data to a tax preparation program called MacInTax, coincidentally also made by Intuit. With federal and state tax forms built in, MacInTax can do a complete job of tax preparation, from helping you find information to calculating and printing your final tax return.

When it comes to taxes, I hate surprises. I use the Quicken Tax Planner to get a ballpark figure for my taxes before I see my accountant.

In this chapter, you'll see how to do some tax planning, create these reports, and get your Quicken data ready for MacInTax.

Planning for Taxes

You can't avoid paying taxes al together, but it's perfectly OK to work hard at finding and using every tax deduction that you can legally claim. Quicken has two tools that you can use to help reduce for tax load: the Tax Deduction Finder, one of the Financial Fitness planners available in Quicken Deluxe 98, and the Quicken Tax Planner, a financial calculator that lets you try out different tax scenarios.

To use the Tax Deduction Finder:

1. Insert the Quicken Deluxe 98 CD in your CD-ROM drive so that you'll be able to experience the Tax Deduction Finder's QuickTime movies and audio help.

2. Choose Activities > Financial Fitness > Tax Deduction Finder. The Tax Deduction Finder's "Getting started" screen appears (**Figure 16.1**).

3. Play each of the three introductory QuickTime movies by clicking the square buttons next to the title of each movie. Then click the Next button. The "Personal info" screen appears (**Figure 16.2**).

4. Fill in the personal information requested in the screen. If you click "Yes" to the question "Are you married?" boxes will appear for you to enter your spouse's information. Click the Next button, and the Deductions introduction screen appears (**Figure 16.3**).

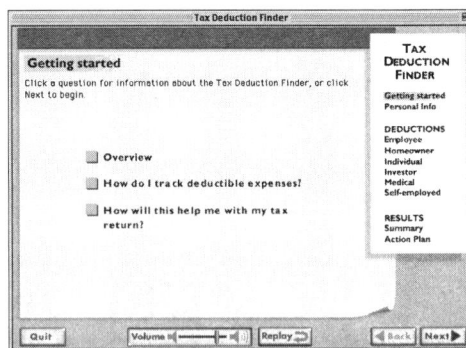

Figure 16.1 Click topics on the "Getting started" screen to watch and hear about Quicken's Tax Deduction Finder.

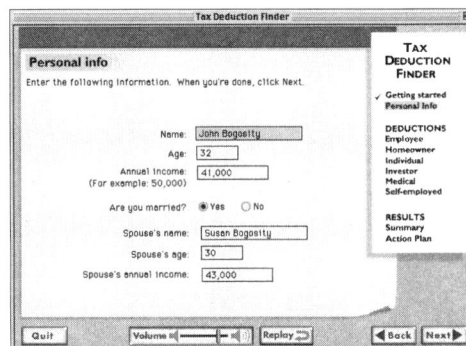

Figure 16.2 Enter information about you and your spouse in this screen.

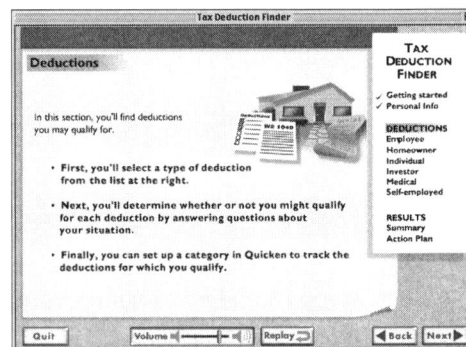

Figure 16.3 Read this screen for information about deductions.

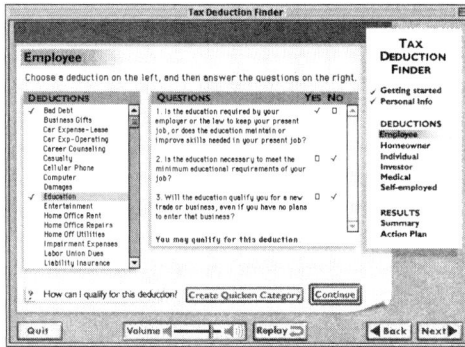

Figure 16.4 Choose a deduction category on the left and answer questions on the right to determine potential tax deductions.

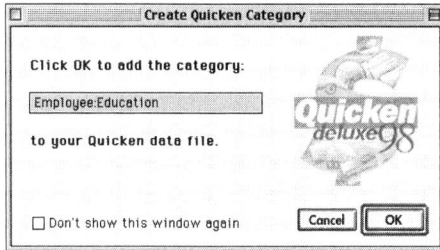

Figure 16.5 Click OK to add a deduction category to your Quicken data file.

5. Read the information the "Deduction" screen, and then click the Next button. The "Employee" screen appears (**Figure 16.4**).

6. The Tax Deduction Finder tests to determine whether you qualify for a particular deduction by asking you a series of questions about each deduction. Select a deduction from the scrolling list on the left side of the screen and, on the right side, click Yes or No to answer each question. The planner will tell you either that you can't take the deduction or that you may be eligible for the deduction.

   If you do possibly qualify for the deduction, the Create Quicken Category window (**Figure 16.5**) appears, asking if you wish to add a category covering the deduction to your Quicken data file. You can edit the name of the proposed category or add the category as listed. Then click the OK button. If you don't want to add the category, click the Cancel button.

7. Continue choosing deductions in the scrolling list on the left side of the screen until you have worked through all the deductions that you think may possibly apply to you. Then click the Next button to go to the next deduction screen ("Homeowner") or click one of the other types in the Deductions area to go directly to that screen.

PLANNING FOR TAXES

8. When you have worked through all of the areas under Deductions, click Results in the menu on the right side of the screen. The "Results" introduction screen appears (**Figure 16.6**). Read the information, and then click the Next button. The "Summary" screen appears (**Figure 16.7**), listing your deduction categories.

9. Review the Summary screen, and then click the Next button. The "Action Plan" screen appears (**Figure 16.8**).

10. If you want a copy of your Action Plan to show to your tax preparer, click the Print button.

✔ Tip

■ The Tax Deduction Finder uses internal information based on the 1997 tax year. Since the tax code changes every year, you'll want to make sure that you check over the recommendations in your Action Plan with your accountant or with another tax professional. Or you can call the Internal Revenue Service with general tax questions at (800)829-1040.

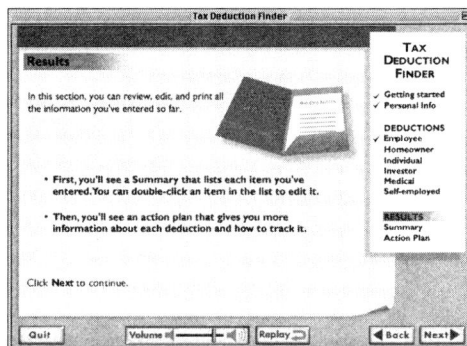

Figure 16.6 Read the information in the Results screen to find out what happens next.

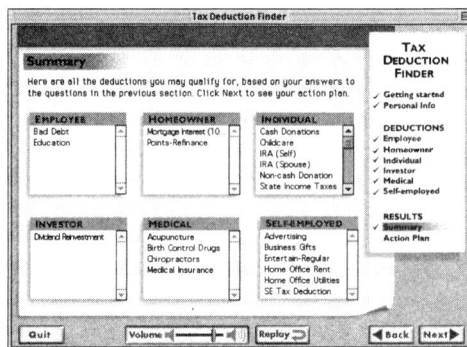

Figure 16.7 You can see a summary of your tax deductions on this screen.

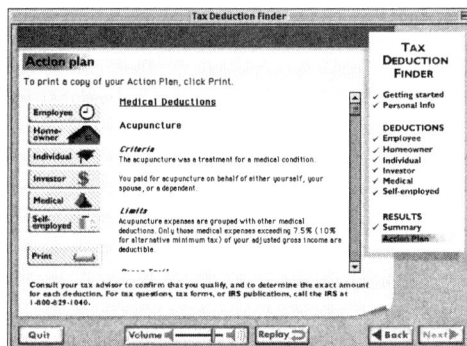

Figure 16.8 Print a copy of your tax deduction action plan for your accountant from this screen.

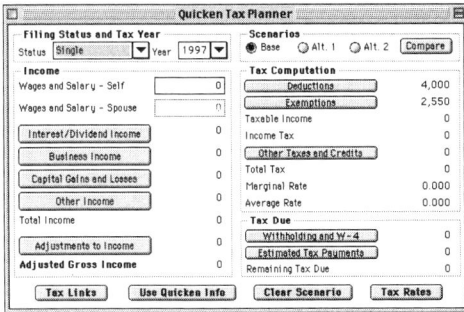

Figure 16.9 In the Quicken Tax Plan Window, click the "Use Quicken Info" button and Quicken will insert your pre-entered data.

To use the Tax Planner:

1. Choose Activities > Planning Calculators > Tax. The Quicken Tax Planner window appears (**Figure 16.9**).

2. Under "Filing Status and Tax Year" at the top of the window, choose your filing status and the tax year from the pop-up menus.

3. Click the "Use Quicken Info" button at the bottom of the window to have the planner import your financial data from the data file.

4. Use the Tax Links button at the bottom of the window to open the Assign Tax Links window, where you can assign Quicken categories to specific line items on federal tax forms.

   For more information about Tax Links, see Chapter 3. (In general, the more Tax Links you assign the better, in terms of the Quicken Tax Planner's accuracy.)

5. You can click any of the buttons in the Income or Tax Computation areas to enter detailed information.

6. After you have entered all your tax information, the tax planner calculates your total tax, which shows you the amount you owe the IRS or the amount of your refund.

✔ Tip

■ If you want to see the tax implications of decisions such as buying a home, or filing taxes jointly or separately, you can try out three different tax scenarios and Quicken will give you the results. Click the Scenarios buttons, fill in the alternate information, and then switch between the tax scenarios to compare how each turns out.

USING THE TAX PLANNER

Creating Tax Reports

Your accountant will probably be interested in four kinds of Quicken reports while preparing your tax return:

- A **Category Summary** report shows the totals for all of your income and expense categories.

- A **Tax Summary** report shows your tax-related income and expenses, subtotaled by category.

- The **Tax Schedule** report groups information from all accounts in your data file that have tax lines assigned to them. The report lists information is grouped by tax form.

- A **Capital Gains** report shows the realized capital gains from your investment accounts.

You create and print each of these reports in almost exactly the same way. (For more information about creating reports, see Chapter 10.)

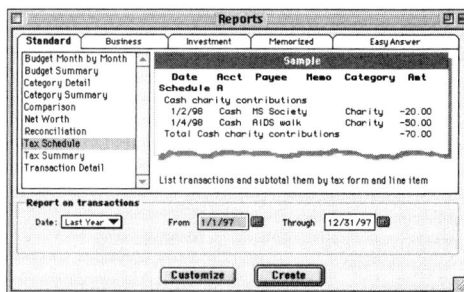

Figure 16.10 You can ask Quicken to create specific tax reports from this window.

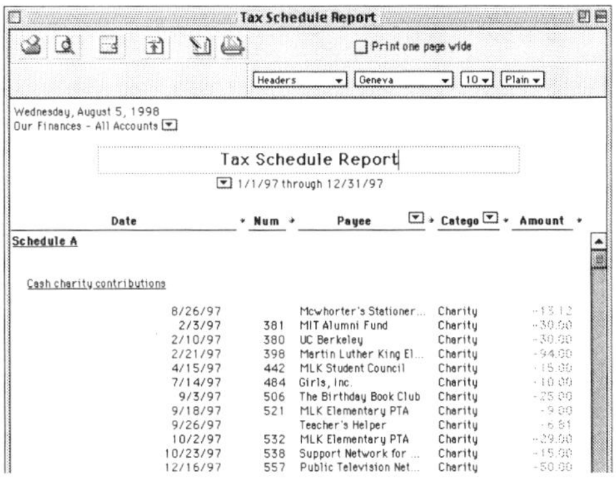

Figure 16.11 This Tax Schedule report shows you the results of your Tax Links, organized by the federal forms to which they pertain.

To create a tax report:

1. Click the Reporting button in the activity bar to get to Quicken's reporting area.

2. Click the Reports button in the task bar to open the Reports window (**Figure 16.10**).

3. Click on the Standard tab in the Reports window, and then click Category Summary, Tax Schedule, or Tax Summary in the scrolling list on the left side of the window.

   Or

   Click on the Investment tab in the Reports window, and then click Capital Gains in the scrolling list on the left side of the window.

4. Change the date range in the bottom of the window to print reports for particular dates, as needed.

5. Click the Create button. Quicken creates and displays the report (**Figure 16.11**).

Exporting Quicken Data to MacInTax

Quicken can save data from a tax schedule report or a capital gains report in a format that's compatible with MacInTax. This format is called Tax Exchange Format (TXF). MacInTax can then read in the TXF file, saving you from having to do a lot of repetitive data entry.

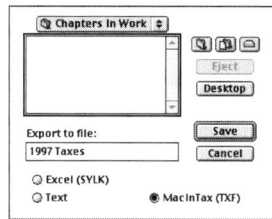

Figure 16.12 For the report to format properly for MacInTax, you must select the MacInTax (TXF) radio button in the Save dialog box.

To export Quicken data:

1. Create the tax report you want to export, and leave it open on your screen.

2. Choose File > Export Report. The standard Save dialog box will appear (**Figure 16.12**).

3. Enter a name for the report file in the "Export to File" box.

4. Click the MacInTax (TXF) button.

5. Click the Save button.

✔ Tip

■ If the MacInTax (TXF) button is dimmed in the Save dialog box, it is probably because you have created a report that isn't a tax schedule or capital gains report and therefore isn't appropriate to send to MacInTax.

USING QUICKEN.COM

To make smart decisions about your finances, you're going to need up-to-date financial and investment information. That's what Quicken.com, Intuit's huge World Wide Web site at http://www.quicken.com is all about.

Quicken.com offers up-to-the-minute news, price quotes, and information about the securities markets; tips from expert financial advisers; access to online stock brokerages; retirement planning tools; and current tax information, including explanations of whatever wacky changes Congress makes in the tax code.

Intuit used to include some of this information, such as a Mutual Fund Finder program, on the Quicken CD-ROM. But the information so quickly became outdated and useless that the company removed the Mutual Fund Finder from the version of Quicken Deluxe 98 that is bundled with the iMac.

The Web site tries to cover every aspect of your financial life by organizing its content into nine departments: Investments, Taxes, Insurance, Home & Mortgage, Retirement Planning, Banking & Borrowing, Saving & Spending, People & Chat, and Small Business.

In this chapter, you'll see how to use some of Quicken.com's financial news and tools. Unfortunately, I barely have room to scratch the surface. I urge you to spend some time browsing the site; it'll be time well spent.

Getting Around on Quicken.com

Before you start browsing the site, you should know what equipment and software you need to view Quicken.com. At a minimum, you'll need the following:

- A Macintosh with a color screen. Your Mac should have a PowerPC or 68040 processor, at least 16 MB of RAM, and it should be running System 7.5 or later.

- A modem or another connection device. If you're using a modem (most people are), its speed should be at least 28.8 kilobits per second. Most modems that are currently being sold are 33.6 Kbits or 56 Kbits per second. If you're lucky enough to have a faster connection to the Internet, such as a cable modem, an ISDN line, or a local area network, so much the better.

- An account with an Internet Service Provider (ISP). An ISP sells access to the Internet. When you sign up with an ISP, you usually get an e-mail account and the ability to create your own Web site, as well as access to all the various Internet services. Many people use America Online as their ISP.

- Web browsing software, such as Netscape Navigator, Netscape Communicator, or Microsoft Internet Explorer.

The process of getting an account with an ISP and signing onto the Internet is beyond the scope of this book, so I will assume you've taken care of that part.

Once you're logged on to the Internet, start up your Web browser and type in http://www.quicken.com, and then press the Return key. You should see something like the screen shown in **Figure 17.1**. If you get to Quicken.com and the screen looks nothing

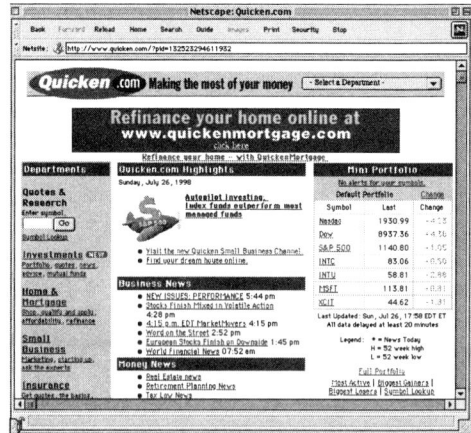

Figure 17.1 When you log on to Quicken.com, this page shows you the way to the site's helpful information.

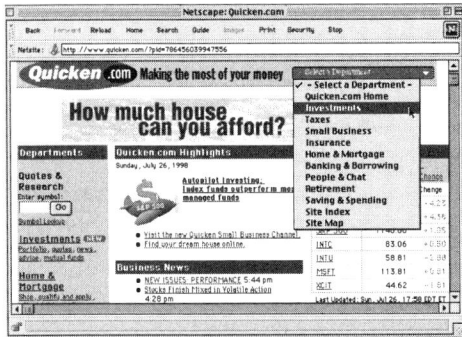

Figure 17.2 Choose one of the departments from this pop-up menu to find specific information.

like **Figure 17.1**, chances are Intuit has redesigned the site since I wrote this book in the summer of 1998. Don't panic; companies are forever changing their Web sites. Just poke around until you find what you're looking for.

Along the left side of the screen, in the Departments navigation bar, you'll see Quicken.com's department names. Click on a name to open that department's page. The middle of the window is taken up by current financial news, and a Mini Portfolio table appears on the right.

At the top of the browser window is a navigation pop-up menu with the legend "Select a Department." Opening this pop-up menu (**Figure 17.2**) to reveal Quicken.com department names. Choose one of the departments from the pop-up menu to tell your browser to go to that department. These are the same Departments found in the navigation bar on the left side of the screen; the difference is that the navigation pop-up menu is available anywhere on the Quicken.com site, whereas the left-side navigation bar changes depending on which Department you're in.

✔ Tips

■ At the bottom of almost all pages on the Quicken.com site are text links that can also take you to any department.

■ You can click the Quicken.com logo at the top of most of the pages on the site to return to the Quicken.com home page.

■ Quicken.com is partners with the Excite Web search engine, so you can search the Web from the Quicken.com home page by entering a search term in the "Search the Web" box at the bottom of the page (not shown in Figure **17.1**).

Finding Investment Information

Quicken.com's Investments department is most often used by most people, and it's the easiest to find. Because it's impossible to discuss everything you could do in the Investments department in the amount of space that I have here, I'll focus on just a few common tasks.

To find a security quote:

1. Select Investments in the navigation pop-up menu at the top of the Quicken.com home page. The Investments page appears (**Figure 17.3**).

2. If you're interested in a quote on a particular security, and you know the security's ticker symbol, type the symbol in the box under "Enter symbol" and click the Go button. A detailed quote page for the security appears (**Figure 17.4**).

3. If you're interested in any other information about the same security, choose it from the links down the left side of the page, under the security's name. For example, after you click the Charts link, you'll see a page like **Figure 17.5**.

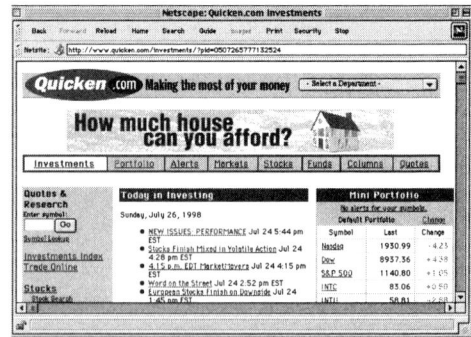

Figure 17.3 Type a stock's symbol in the box under "Enter symbol" and click the Go button to see information about a particular security.

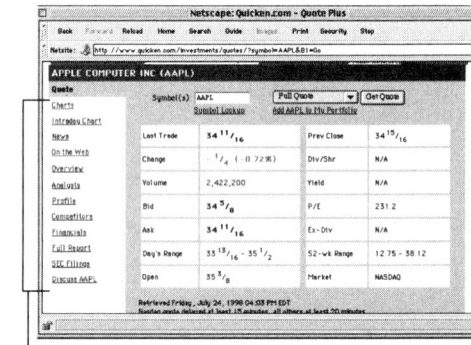

Detail links

Figure 17.4 You can check out details about a security on this quotes page.

Figure 17.5 Click the Charts link on the quotes page to see a chart of the security, like this one.

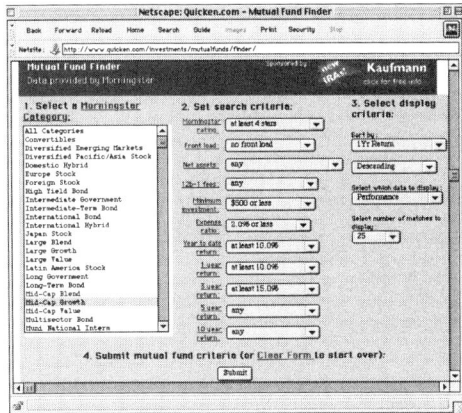

Figure 17.6 You can get information about a particular mutual fund from this page.

Figure 17.7 Check out the Mutual Fund Finder page to see results of your search.

To find a mutual fund:

Thousands of mutual funds are available, and each fund has its own investment objectives. Selecting a mutual fund that meets your criteria for investment is fairly easy using Quicken.com, because it contains detailed information on virtually all funds.

1. From the main Investments page (shown in **Figure 17.3**), scroll down and click "Fund Finder" under Mutual Funds. The Mutual Fund Finder page appears (**Figure 17.6**).

2. In the scrolling list on the left side of the window, click a category to select it.

3. Under "Set search criteria," choose your search criteria using the pop-up menus. If you don't understand a particular criteria term, click on its name to jump to an explanation screen. When you're done reading the explanation, click your browser's Back button to return to the Mutual Fund Finder.

4. Under "Select display criteria," use the pop-up menus to choose the way that you want to view the report that will be created.

5. Click the Submit button at the bottom of the page. The Mutual Fund Finder will show the results of your search (**Figure 17.7**).

To get answers to basic questions about investing:

Investing can be confusing. The terminology is often complex, with arcane terms, weird acronyms, and convoluted explanations. Do you know what an index fund is? Why is Morningstar important? What does it mean to sell a stock short? Are DRIPs good for you? Thankfully, Quicken.com has a place where these questions can get answers.

1. In the main Investments page, scroll down and click "Basics." The main Investing Basics page will appear (**Figure 17.8**).

2. In the navigation bar on the left side of the page, click QuickAnswers. The QuickAnswers page appears (**Figure 17.9**).

3. Find the question that you want answered in the QuickAnswers list, and then click on the question to jump to that question's answer page. If you can't find the question that you want answered in the list, look through the Related Links navigation bar on the left side of the page for a section of the site that might help you.

Figure 17.8 Use the navigation bar on the main Investing Basics page to get quick answers to your questions.

Figure 17.9 Find the question that you want answered in the QuickAnswers list.

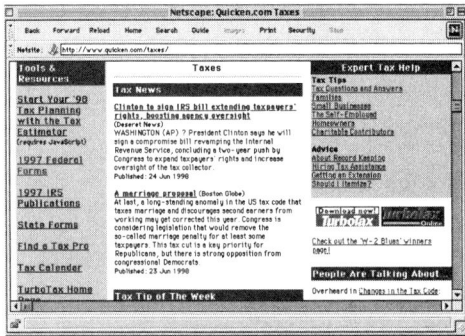

Figure 17.10 Find the category of information that you need from the main Taxes page.

Figure 17.11 Click a tax form to download it from this page.

Getting Tax Information

The more information you have about taxes, the more likely you'll make intelligent decisions when tax time comes. The Taxes section of Quicken.com has a lot of general tax information and a tax estimating tool—and you can even download federal and state tax forms from the site.

To find tax tips and advice:

1. From the main Investments page, scroll down and click "Taxes." The main Taxes page will appear (**Figure 17.10**).

2. Under the heading on the right side of the page entitled "Expert Tax Help," find the category of information that you need, and then click on that category to jump to an information page.

To download tax forms:

Quicken.com lets you download to your computer federal and state tax forms. You can then print these forms and use them to file your taxes. The files are in Adobe Acrobat format (sometimes called PDF files, for Portable Document Format). To read Acrobat files, you'll need to install the free Acrobat Reader program. It comes on the Quicken Deluxe 98 CD-ROM, or you can download it from Adobe's Web site at http://www.adobe.com.

1. In the navigation bar on the left side of the main Taxes page, click the link "1997 Federal Forms." If you're reading this in 1999, the link will be called "1998 Federal Forms." The Forms page will appear (**Figure 17.11**).

2. Scroll down the list until you find the tax form or forms that you want to download. Click on the title of a form to begin the download to your hard disk.

Finding Low-Rate Credit Cards

Credit cards are handy to use, but they can be a major source of financial frivolity. If you don't pay your credit card balance off in full every month, you rack up interest charges. If you can't avoid running a balance, you can at least try to minimize the amount of interest you're paying by finding a credit card with a low interest rate.

Quicken.com's Banking & Borrowing area has a list of the cheapest credit card providers as well as other useful information, such as mortgage interest rates, savings account interest yields, and general banking information.

To find the cheapest credit cards:

1. From the main Investments page, choose "Banking & Borrowing" from the navigation bar on the left. The main Banking & Borrowing page appears (**Figure 17.12**).

2. In the navigation bar on the left, click "Best deals" under Credit Cards. The Bank Rate Monitor page appears (**Figure 17.13**).

3. Answer the questions about your objective, what type of card you want, the class of card (classic, gold, platinum) you want, and how many responses you want. Then click the Go button.

4. The results screen appears, based on the search criteria you gave in step 3.

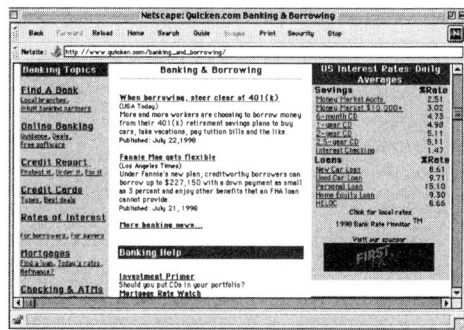

Figure 17.12 In the navigation bar on the left of this page, click "Best deals" under Credit Cards to open the Bank Rate Monitor page.

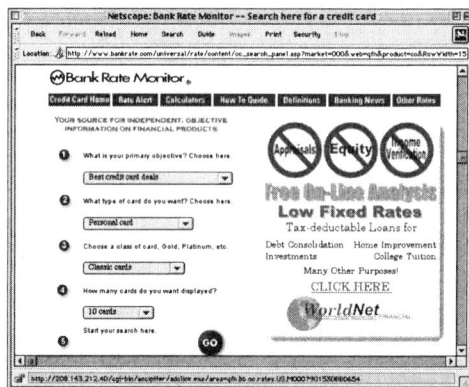

Figure 17.13 Indicate your requirements, and then click Go to start the search for the best credit card and bank rates.

INDEX

INDEX